by Arthur Goodfriend:

IF YOU WERE BORN IN RUSSIA

THE ONLY WAR WE SEEK . . .

WHAT CAN A MAN BELIEVE?

WHAT CAN A MAN DO?

SOMETHING IS MISSING . . .

WHAT IS AMERICA?

STAND FAST IN LIBERTY

State Department Publications:

WHEN THE COMMUNISTS CAME

TWO SIDES OF ONE WORLD

PATHS OF ACTION TOWARD ASIAN-AMERICAN UNDER-
STANDING AND COOPERATION

INDONESIA: A CASE STUDY IN ASIAN-AMERICAN UNDER-
STANDING

Rice Roots

by
Arthur Goodfriend

WITH PHOTOGRAPHS BY BAMBANG

SIMON AND SCHUSTER
NEW YORK, 1958

FIRST PRINTING

LIBRARY OF CONGRESS CATALOG CARD NUMBER: 58-11817
MANUFACTURED IN THE UNITED STATES OF AMERICA
BY AMERICAN BOOK-STRATFORD PRESS, INC., NEW YORK

To Slamet, Bambang, Muljono, Djonny
and other Indonesian friends
who will recognize themselves
and their contribution to these pages
even though, in certain cases
and for reasons they understand,
their names have been changed.

Contents

Human understanding that transcends national and ideological borders is the truest path to enduring peace.

—Dwight D. Eisenhower

Rice Roots

ONE

First Steps
Toward Understanding

T HIS BOOK deals with an Asian people, the Indonesians. It
is not written just because Indonesia is among the Asian
nations most recently gripped by crisis. Nor does it deal directly
and solely with Indonesia's crisis. It is written, rather, to probe
the causes and conditions underlying Asia's incessant crises—
and because Indonesia, perhaps better than any other Asian
land, offers Americans an insight into all of Asia, and into
their own role, responsibility and opportunity in Asia's future.

For Indonesia and its people are an archetype of Asia. Here
geography and history have fused almost every Asian strain.
Here are Malayan blood, Buddhist art, Hindu scripture, Islam's
God. Here are every Asian woe and every Asian hope. Here are
Asia's "teeming masses"—poor, proud, and infinitely powerful.
Here, incarnate, are Asia's rice roots.

The existence and nature of these, the rice roots, are but
vaguely sensed or understood. Mute, innumerable, anonymous
and passive until suddenly whipped into turbulence by the
wind of events—Asia's masses frustrate Western comprehen-

3

sion. Important, they continue inscrutable, they remain unknown.

It is not, then, on parliaments and politicians, or on revolution and civil strife, or on Asia's other overt aspects, but on these, the hidden rice roots, that these pages dwell. For it is at the rice roots that Asia's great men and great causes are nourished. It is here, at the rice roots, that America's understanding of Asia might well begin.

My own understanding of Asia began elsewhere, in a police court in Peiping. It was 1935. Cruise ships disgorged Western wares and wanderers like myself in the bazaars of the East and swallowed huge cargoes of tea, rubber, teak and tin. Like others, entranced with what the literature of the time labeled "the lure of the East," I was blind to all that seethed beneath the colonial calm. India seemed a stalwart prop beneath the British raj. The French seemed successfully to be molding Indochina in their graceful image. A handful of Hollanders appeared to have eighty million picturesque natives of the Netherlands East Indies under their thumb. Of the "natives" themselves—of their unspeakable humiliation, of their frustration, of the nationalist fever shaking Asia from Shanghai to Suez—I was supremely unaware. Of their subtlety, their sophistication, their pride I had no hint—until that evening in Peiping.

With another touring American I had gone to a restaurant in the old city to taste the highly touted Heavenly Duck. A stiff breeze was blowing off the desert, and we invited our rickshaw coolies inside for warmth. They squatted by a wall while we sipped hot wine and waited for our dinner. It began to arrive

4

in small, untempting fragments, which we offered to the boys.

My companion's rickshaw boy was a Moslem who would eat nothing prepared with pork. Mine wolfed down an almost endless succession of pancakes and dumplings, sauces and soups, gizzards and skin which we vainly searched for signs of duck and passed on to him. After a long pause signalizing, we hoped, the appearance of an edible drumstick, the waiter arrived with our bill. The Heavenly Duck, we realized too late, had been completely consumed by my boy.

Disappointed and hungry, we paid and asked the coolies to take us back to our hotel. The Moslem, with his passenger, disappeared down the street before my boy could squeeze between the shafts of his rickshaw. The boy staggered a few steps and collapsed, clutching his swollen stomach. I was at an age when the solution to the crisis was easy. Placing him in the rickshaw, I picked up the shafts and started to run.

The spectacle of a foreigner pulling a rickshaw created a stir. Other coolies trotted delightedly beside me, followed by a horde of howling children. I quickly acquired the knack of resting my elbows on the shafts, letting momentum drive the sensitively balanced vehicle forward. Making excellent time, we wheeled into Hata Men, the main street. I was outracing the procession when, at an intersection, a policeman waved me to a stop.

In pidgin English I explained that the coolie had eaten an entire duck and was too sick to pull the rickshaw. The constable nodded sympathetically but motioned me to follow him. A crowd accompanied us to the nearby police court, a shabby, dimly lit establishment devoted principally to settling the fates of pickpockets and prostitutes. A walnut of a man, brown, round and wrinkled, presided. He ordered silence and listened to the constable's account. Several other witnesses also testified.

5

I awaited my turn, confident that my explanation would win acquittal.

The magistrate acted as if I didn't exist. The hearing completed, a clerk took my arm and led me to a bench. Angry at my public humiliation, I waited while he filled in a set of forms. After stamping each page with a chop, he held up the fingers of one hand and said, "Fi' dollar mex."

A Mexican dollar, the specie of the time, was worth about twenty-five cents. I paid the money indignantly and received a receipt. My rickshaw boy, fully recovered, returned me to the hotel, too late for supper. But the bar was open and I ordered a pink gin. "Master angry," the bar boy said. I nodded and told him what had happened. "And here," I concluded, "is the receipt for the fine. I am keeping it as a souvenir of Chinese justice."

The bar boy picked up the piece of paper and held it to the light. "But, master," he said, after long, careful study, "this is not receipt for fine. This license to pull rickshaw."

That evening I learned respect for Asians.

Ten years later, in 1945, I learned to admire them.

I had served in Europe as editor of the Army's newspaper, the *Stars and Stripes*. V-E day brought orders sending me to Chungking to set up an edition in the China theater. When Shanghai was liberated I flew down with two ace GI correspondents, Ed Hogan and Johnny Clift, and took over the plant of the old *China Post*. It was partially wrecked, and what equipment remained intact seemed hopelessly primitive. We stared glumly at the mess. Even if we managed to start the antique, battered press, we had neither newsprint, ink nor lead. The troops pouring into Shanghai after months in the interior, famished for news among other things, would have a long wait for Li'l Abner and Daisy Mae.

Miraculously, two emaciated Chinese, prewar *Post* staffers, came to the rescue. Toothless and bald, they resembled the Dowager Empress' eunuchs. Neither spoke a word of English, but they could click off copy on the linotype and run the press. In three days they tidied up the shop, assorted the type and cranked the machine. It took them one more day to scrounge enough paper, ink and metal for a first edition.

We made ready to roll. Type, locked in forms, lay on the composing-room stone. The press warmed up with a reassuring clatter. A jeep stood by to rush the edition to the Yangtze docks where the Seventh Fleet had just anchored. It was time to convert the type forms into printing plates and produce some papers. We looked around for mats.

Mats are sheets of heavy, specially treated cardboard which, pressed against type, form a matrix. Into the matrix molten metal is poured to form the block from which the paper is printed. We had no mats.

Hogan, Clift and I cursed ourselves for overlooking the small but crucial detail. The two eunuchs remained unruffled. They stacked up a sheaf of old newspapers, soaked them in water, dusted them with rice flour, rolled the powdered pulp like a piecrust against the type, and placed the package inside an oven. A stench as of burning bread pervaded the press room. After fifteen minutes they took out the mess, charred and smoking, but baked into a perfect mat.

An hour later, copies of the *Stripes* were handed out to cheering troops on Nanking Road. Admiral Kincaid dined us on his flagship. General Wedemeyer pinned a commendation ribbon on my breast. Neither the General, the Admiral nor twenty thousand soldiers and sailors knew it, but they owed their newspapers to two Asian craftsmen who, all their lives, had learned to make do with very little.

In 1945, too, I sensed the power of Asia, aroused and on the march. For to me fell the dubious distinction of being one of the first American soldiers to fall into a Communist army's hands.

Somewhere north of Peiping, an oasis in the desert was garrisoned by a detachment of United States Marines. Once a week a convoy took out supplies and mail. I went along on one trip to deliver the *Stripes*. Commanded by a young redheaded major, the party consisted of a Chinese interpreter and twenty marines armed with carbines and traveling in five weapons carriers and a jeep. We had orders to report anything unusual on our transmitter. The Japanese in the area had surrendered, but rumor had it that a Communist route army was somewhere about, tearing up communications and terrorizing the towns.

Aside from a few road blocks, unmanned and easily bypassed, the outward trip was smooth. We reached the garrison at noon, dumped our cargo and turned around. The desert was dangerous after dark, and the jeep set a fast pace back. The driver shifted into second gear once, to climb one of the few hills dominating the flat wasteland. He reached the top and braked.

A mile off, like a python writhing across the horizon, moved an endless file of troops. Nearer, from the surrounding dunes, the muzzles of rifles pointed at us. The major, the interpreter and I leaped from the jeep and, arms upraised, walked toward the ambush. Khaki-capped heads emerged above the rifles. One man stood up and beckoned to us. We saw the hammer and sickle on his breast and knew we had stumbled into the Communist Army.

The major told the interpreter to say we were in a hurry to reach Peiping before nightfall and wanted a safe-conduct through the line. The Communist shook his head. He said he would have to ask for orders—either to hold us there until the army passed, or to take us along as prisoners. The major said he would fight before submitting to delay or capture. The Communist shrugged. The radio operator walked over and whispered in the major's ear. The major turned to me. "Colonel," he said, "the transmitter's broken. Will you take the interpreter, find their headquarters and talk them into letting us through? If you're not back in an hour, we'll start to shoot."

The Communist assigned us two escorts. One covered us from behind. The other led us into a series of gullies I hadn't noticed on the outward trip. I began to see the main body of the army. I had seen many armies in the past ten years—the German Army goose-stepping down Unter den Linden in its prewar grandeur, the cream of the British Army at an Aldershot Tattoo, the American juggernaut we had flung across the Channel. I had never seen an army like this. It was an army without a wheel, a motor, a horse. It had neither artillery, tanks, trucks nor planes. It was a silent, straggling, primitive horde of human beings, yet, somehow, utterly inhuman, like something dropped from Mars. Possibly fifty thousand men surrounded us. A blind man would not have known they were there.

Twenty minutes of my precious hour elapsed before we found an officer. A stony midget of a man, he took ten minutes more to denounce American meddling in China. I tried to set him straight, without success, then asked permission to cut across his column. He thought for an eternity and finally consented, provided that his men covered our drivers during the passage. I glanced at my watch and agreed.

When I dropped down beside the major, scant seconds before the deadline, his blouse was black with sweat. We remounted and, with deadpan Communist privates clinging to our windshields, approached the thin black line. A section halted as we crossed its path. The desert-stained faces were blank. The bodies were gaunt. The quilted cotton uniforms were tattered, the equipment was nondescript and sparse. Only the rifles looked new and clean.

"Good God," said the major. "Garands!"

That night, in the bar of the Wagons-Lits hotel, the major and I parted. He proved to be something of a prophet.

"Colonel," he said, "we were lucky. It would have been one hell of a job for twenty marines to beat a whole Red army."

I learned another Asian lesson in 1949. Peiping, along with all of northern China, lay in communism's grip. The Nationalists were making one of their notorious last stands on a line covering Kwantung, Kwangsi and Szechwan provinces. Below, a splinter of America's ECA was striving to prop free China. It had a typical bureaucratic tongue-twister of a name, the Joint Commission on Rural Reconstruction. When I received an invitation to fly to Canton and join its ranks, I seized it. Even in 1949 China held for me its old allure—color, excitement, an aura of romance.

Canton didn't disappoint me. The arcades around the Oikwan, an ultramodern skyscraper hotel, were a vast encampment of Nationalist wounded, who tugged at my trousers and begged for alms. The lobby was thronged with wealthy fugitives and beggars and pimps. I checked in and squeezed into the crowded elevator. As it rose, a silent struggle shook the cage. The elevator emptied at the twentieth floor, except for a huddled body bleeding on the floor. In the corridor burly bodyguards posted outside doors eyed me dourly. Inside my room, stretched on the bed, lay a slit-skirted girl who offered to spend the night for a dollar. After she left I called the clerk and told him there was a corpse in the elevator. He giggled nervously and said he was sorry. Canton had what I had come for—color, excitement, an aura of romance.

Next morning, at their headquarters on the island of Shameen, I met the commissioners. The chief was Dr. Chiang Mon-lin, thin, tall, with the eyes and smile of a saint. We reminisced about Peiping, where he had been Minister of Education. He introduced me to his associates, fiery little Jimmy Yen, father of China's mass-education movement, and Dr. Shen Tsung-han, the nation's leading plant-breeding specialist. The Americans were Dr. Raymond T. Moyer, a gentle-mannered veteran of fifteen years' agricultural work at Oberlin-in-Shansi, and Dr. John Earl Baker, former director of International Famine Relief in China.

These five men, aided by a small staff of Chinese and American technicians, were pitted against forces generated by centuries of social injustice. Driven from Peiping and Shanghai, they labored here, in the sweatbath of South China, amid runaway inflation and civil war, for better crops, clinics and schools in the villages. For their work, Congress had allotted thirty million dollars.

Ray Moyer described my job. He talked about a disease called rinderpest. "It kills thousands of water buffalo every year. The buffalo is the power plant of the Chinese farm. When it dies, the farmer's hope dies with it. We want to save the cattle by injecting them with a serum made from the spleen of

11

infected rabbits. The people are afraid of it. Your job is to explain our methods and results in pictures and posters illiterate folk can understand."

It seemed to me we should be fighting Reds, not rinderpest. But I did what I was told. I watched inoculation teams at work in the villages, listened to farmers' questions, sketched the answers and printed up charts describing graphically rinderpest's causes and cure. We posted them on village walls, in town halls, in market places. A few farmers peered at them quizzically and walked away. I was baffled and hurt. Chiang Monlin consoled me. "You are on the right track," he said, studying my charts through rimless glasses. "Here in China we invented the saying that one picture is worth a thousand words. But," he added, almost apologetically, "perhaps the picture must be Chinese."

My Asian education leaped a long step forward. In a newspaper office in Canton I discovered the Al Capp of South China, a gangling lad named Lee. Lee invented a little character named Happy Boy, a pigtailed tot dressed in the conveniently open-bottomed trousers affected by Chinese youngsters. Happy Boy was portrayed as almost losing his cow to rinderpest, then saving him with serum. He made a hit. Petitions for serum reached the commission. When a rinderpest epidemic scourged Kwantung, results spoke for themselves. In one area where no cattle had been injected, three thousand buffalo died, three thousand families were ruined. In an adjacent area, where all cattle had been treated, every animal lived. The cost per cow was less than a penny. It was a revelation to me as much as to the farmers.

Happy Boy went on to pictorialize the commission's work in hog cholera, seed multiplication, irrigation, flood control, farmers' co-operatives, rural health. Benefits were perceptible to the

12

most myopic farmer. Popular confidence grew and provided a base for assault on China's age-old evils—landlessness, tenancy, usury. Ninety per cent of the land was owned by four per cent of the people. Tillers rented land at rates in excess of 75 per cent of the crop. The commission prevailed on provincial governments to slash rents to 37.5 per cent. In Kwangsi and Szechwan, five million families held up their heads.

It was just a beginning, born in crisis. But in five months the root causes of unrest withered. The cost to the American taxpayer was nine cents for each family helped. The list of little victories was long, but the big victory eluded us. One September morning we were awakened by rifle fire in the suburbs. Silently, sadly, we packed and flew to Formosa.

A rear-guard action had failed to save China. But from defeat emerged the first, faint outline of a strategy that, grasped and applied in time, might save the rest of Asia.

In the darkness of the debacle, I learned there was hope.

Homeward bound, months later, I wondered how a private citizen without political influence could invade the White House, the State Department, the Capitol and tell what he had learned in China. The idea was presumptuous, but it persisted. Somehow, I wanted to bring the President of the United States face to face with the farmers and workers of Asia, their problems, their hopes, and America's best answer. But how?

It occurred to me that the President and the peasants might share a common trait—willingness to believe the vivid evidence of pictures. The publishers of *Life* magazine, to whom I described my purpose, agreed and opened to me their photographic archives. The result was a mammoth picture portfolio weighing ninety pounds, a self-easeled contraption which, once set up on the President's desk, he could neither overlook, nor push aside, nor file away. I called it "Through Chinese Eyes."

The only remaining problem was to get the portfolio onto the President's desk. On the train to Washington, the optimism generated in the heat of creation vanished. In the entire capital I knew scarcely a soul, certainly no one with sufficient leverage to hoist me into the White House. For lack of a better plan I decided on an oblique attack via the State Department. In the lobby of its offices in Foggy Bottom I scanned the directory for a clue. Sighting an Assistant Secretary of State for Southeast Asia, I headed for his office. A receptionist asked if I had an appointment. I said I didn't, pointed to the package, and explained my mission. She regretted that the Assistant Secretary was tied up, but *his* assistant, down the hall, would doubtless be delighted to hear my views on Asia.

The assistant proved equally busy. His secretary suggested a third assistant, farther down the hall. I traveled farther and farther, down more and more distant halls until, after two weeks of courteous brushoffs, I found myself in the remote environs of the District of Columbia with nowhere else to go. In despair I turned to Ernest K. Lindley, the *Newsweek* columnist. He didn't know me from any other subscriber, but he set aside Saturday morning to look and listen. He called me the following Monday and said the Assistant Secretary of State for Southeast Asia wanted to see me.

The portfolio suddenly acquired a respectable status. Senators asked for a showing. General Vaughn approved it. A member of the President's brain trust took it under his wing. So did Dean Acheson. Three weeks after the siege had been laid, the telephone rang by my bedside. "The President," said a voice at the other end, "would appreciate seeing 'Through Chinese Eyes.'"

Harry Truman strode into the Cabinet Room, sat down and folded his arms. Light glinted on his glasses, hiding his eyes, but his lips stretched thin as I turned the pages.

The theme was simple but, in 1950, novel. Dollars and diplomacy might reach Asian governments, but they were not reaching the people. Much that we were doing was far removed from their grievances, anxieties, needs and hopes. Only by getting down in the dirt and working beside them, on equal terms, toward goals the people understood and cherished, could we win their friendship. Only by knowing their goals and identifying our own with theirs could we persuade Asians to join us in their achievement. Only Asians with something to defend, and the will to defend it, could save Asia. Billions spent in Asia to reshape it in America's image would be wasted. But pennies spent to strengthen Asia's own indigenous institutions, to build improvements the people themselves could pay for and maintain, would help create the self-respect, self-reliance, self-confidence indispensable to prosperity, freedom, and peace in Asia. America, in short, should shift its sights from Asia's leaders, many of them discredited, to Asia's masses.

When I finished, the President sat silent for several seconds. Then he said, "You are right. The lesson is clear. We must apply it to the rest of Asia before it is too late. But the load is on the shoulders of the man in the street. Tell him what you've just told me."

I took the President's advice. The portfolio, converted into a thin volume, sold more than a hundred thousand copies. Invitations to speak arrived from civic groups, women's clubs, political organizations. I leaped at the chance to proselytize my fellow Americans.

It turned out, instead, that my audiences proselytized me. Somehow, my message was subtly twisted. Somewhere in that public-speaking tour, emphasis shifted from what had seemed right in Asia to something that seemed right in America. Pity for Asians. Confidence that material means could gain political ends. A determination to give, to spend, to crusade. To *sell* Asia something took precedence. Democracy, some called it. Or freedom. Or a higher living standard. Or free enterprise.

The State Department called it Truth. It embarked on a "Campaign of Truth." When Edward Barrett, Assistant Secretary of State for Public Affairs, asked me to go back to Asia and help put the campaign across, I consented.

That was 1950. That was when I learned about the allure of easy solutions to the Asian enigma: The full rice bowl is the answer to communism. . . . We have the money, the machinery, the know-how to fill it! . . . We must win the minds and hearts of Asia. . . . We must, we can succeed. . . . After all, Americans *are* the world's best salesmen!

My next Asian visit was at a time of mounting crisis. War raged in Korea. The Huks were riding high in the Philippines. Burma teetered on the brink of anarchy. Indonesia had barely quelled a Communist revolt. The tide was running out in Indochina. India's face was freezing in a neutralist mask. All across Asia, America faced frustration and defeat.

Except in Korea, America was fighting back with buckshot. Here and there, tiny outposts of technicians fought valiant battles and scored tactical successes. The main counterattack consisted of words. By Congressional mandate, America had been trying to win over Asia's masses with "a full, fair picture" of its wealth, its productivity, its high standard of living. At my first stop, Manila, Ambassador Myron Cowan pointed almost tearfully at his desk, piled with American propaganda.

"Read it!" he demanded. "We boast about our skyscrapers, automobiles and freezers to barefoot farmers. We flaunt our supermarkets before women whose babies are starving at their breasts. We print the Declaration of Independence in eight-point type and distribute it to illiterates. We fill their movies with the exploits of our Air Force, while communism flies doves of peace. We high-pressure them, scare them, scold them. Then we wonder why they hate our guts!"

The Ambassador cheered the switch from the "full, fair picture" to the "Campaign of Truth." So did the dedicated American officials I met in every Asian country. A search began for Asian heroes, stories and songs that, better than our own, expressed Asia's longing for freedom. Pamphlets, cartoon booklets, local broadcasts, originating in Asia rather than in Washington, echoed Asian values in Asian symbols and sounds. To link the truest, deepest of those values with our own, to preach a common struggle against a common enemy and toward common goals became the aim.

Habit was hard to break. Nor do Americans bend easily into Eastern postures. Nevertheless, America began to turn a new face to Asia—a face less smooth, less hard, less self-centered, a face worn with some of the same griefs, fears and longings that marked the faces of those who beheld it. It was altogether a better face. But perceptive Asians saw a blemish.

One such Asian was a Buddhist priest in Thailand. He asked why I had come to visit his temple. I said I sought the enduring truths that bound his people and mine together. With closed eyes he pondered my answer. "Truth," he said, "is a flower. It

17

has purity and beauty. It blooms in the sun. But when man wreathes it into a blandishment, it withers. When he uses it to serve his ends, its fragrance vanishes. When man plucks truth, it dies."

Another was an Indian farmer. "Truth?" he asked. "What is truth? You say truth is one thing. The Communists say truth is another. I think truth is not what men say, but what they do."

Another was a newspaper editor in Indonesia. "America," he said, "bases the case against communism on its own Western ethic. We will never join a crusade which does not defend our own religious convictions." I gave him a copy of one of our newer effusions, quoting the East's religious leaders as well as the West's, and contrasting their philosophies with that of Marx and Lenin. For those who could not read, the faces of Buddha, Confucius, Mohammed and Christ were shown in their benignity, and opposed to the sinister visages of Stalin and Molotov. Opposite the Communist Manifesto were arranged the Bible, the Gita, the Analects, the Koran. Confident that at long last an Asian argument was answered, I awaited his comment.

It came next day in a note clipped to the pamphlet. "Nothing," it read, "is more abhorrent to a Moslem than to print a picture of the Prophet. Nor do we consider it respectful to reproduce the Koran upside down. America knows wealth, science, power, but it does not know the Asian people."

It was, perhaps, too broad an indictment. But deep within me I sensed he was right. America, using strictly its own devices and concepts, was attempting to cope with human forces it did not fully comprehend. America, born of the proposition that governments derive their just powers from the consent of the governed, did not really know the governed, the masses, of Asia. Until it stopped pretending, until it did know the forces that made them and moved them, it could never reach them.

Of my own ignorance I was sure. Over nineteen years, as a businessman, a soldier, an ECA aide, a State Department consultant, I had seen Asians change from vassals to free men. I had seen some of them revert to slavery more cruel than any they had known before. I had learned to respect and admire Asians, to value them as friends, to fear them as enemies. I had worked beside them. I had learned the folly of trying to propagandize them, even in the name of truth.

But I didn't know the Asian people. I had stood at their threshold, but I had never entered the door. I had never risen with them before daybreak and followed them through an Asian day. I had never guided a buffalo through the mud of a paddy field. I had never sat by their fires, partaking of their rice and talk. I had never shared an Asian life from the moment of birth, through infancy, adolescence, maturity, to the coming of death. I knew little of what lay beneath Asia's surface, down deep at the rice roots. I wanted to find out.

Now, with my wife and our two children, I was going back to live among, to learn about, an Asian people. In my pocket was a Rockefeller grant. Its terms were challenging:

Live at the rice roots, among the farmers and workers. Mingle with the youth. Learn how they think and act. Know their problems and fears. See American policies and actions from their viewpoint. Share what you learn with the American people so that we may, perhaps, behave toward Asians with better knowledge of their nature, needs and hopes.

It was to be my fifth trip to Asia. More than any of the others, I wanted this one to succeed.

19

TWO

"Irian or War!"

THE CONSUL'S EYES matched the tortoise shell of his glasses. After scanning our visa applications, they rested briefly on my wife, Eadie, and on me. Then their glance descended toward the children, Jill, age nine, and Arthur, three. Smiling, they focused on the little girl, who was poised on the edge of the chair beside his desk. "Tell me, young lady, why do you want to go to Indonesia?"

Jill had been a silent participant in the discussions leading to our decision. What she had gathered from our talk we had no idea. We awaited her reply with as much interest as the consul. "Because," we heard her say, "the United States and Indonesia are alike. We were once ruled by the English and you were ruled by the Dutch. The difference is, we threw them out a long time ago. Now we need your spices for our cookies and your tin for our tin cans and your rubber for our bubble gum. That's why we want to go to Indonesia and make friends. Without bubble gum we'd die!"

The consul reached down and shook her hand. "Never," he said, "have I heard America's position stated so clearly." Turning to me, he added, "Djakarta will want to know a little more.

20

Why, with almost all of Asia to choose from, have you honored Indonesia?"

There were many reasons. Babies, for one. Thirty out of every hundred Indonesian babies died within a year of their birth. Nowhere else in Asia were infant birth and death rates so catastrophically high. To find out what such tragedy meant to Asian mothers and fathers, to learn what it means to live in a country with one doctor for sixty thousand souls, Indonesia seemed the ideal place.

Poverty, for a second. Seven out of ten Indonesians, like most Asians, were farmers. Their tools had hardly changed in centuries. Their incomes rarely rose above forty dollars a year. To learn what it is like to get along on an Asian income—and how that income might be raised—Indonesia seemed a likely place.

Illiteracy, for a third. Seven in ten Indonesians, prior to 1942, could neither read nor write. Yet these people were trying to build a modern state. They would soon be going to the polls to elect their leaders, to set their country's course. Dissidence, revolution, civil war were ever imminent. Nowhere else was there such a chance to plumb an Asian people's inner thoughts on the eve of such events.

Neutralism, for a fourth. Indonesia had had to fight for its freedom. The scars of battle had not healed. Nowhere in free Asia were suspicion and fear of the West more deeply imbedded. Though short of capital, know-how and equipment, Indonesians had toppled a Cabinet for accepting American aid tied to military conditions. Nowhere in Asia did so much need call more for Western help. Nowhere was it more frustrated by neutralism.

Communism, for a fifth. Indonesia lay only four hundred miles from Red China. It was honeycombed by overseas Chinese, rich, industrious, controlling its commerce, of doubtful loyalty. Its Communist Party, active, alert, was infiltrating the government. Its people, attuned by centuries of serfdom to paternalism were, according to many experts, passive toward democratic self-rule and ripe for Communist picking. Sukarno, the President, seemed utterly indifferent to the danger. What better country in which to observe Communist tactics and prospects than Indonesia? Or to examine America's counterstrategy?

Indonesia's wealth was another reason. Only the United States and the Soviet Union surpassed it in natural resources. Its current exports of oil, rubber, tin, tea, kapok, spice, rice, palm oil and other coconut products placed Indonesia among the most productive of Asian economies. Yet no one knew how much coal, bauxite, uranium, manganese, copper, nickel, silver and gold lay buried in her mountains, or what wealth modern techniques might extract from her rivers, coastal waters, virgin forests and countless acres of unbroken soil. Of all Asia's resources, material and human, none was less known and more worth knowing than Indonesia's.

And finally, culture. Indonesians were linked by religion with the Moslem world, by literature and art with the Hindu, by language and blood with the Malay, by history with the Buddhist, by commerce with the Chinese. Every country and people in Asia, I knew, was different and distinct. But nowhere, in the time available, could I learn so much about Asians generally as in Indonesia.

There were all these reasons and more. But I lacked Jill's felicity. While I struggled to put them into words, Eadie answered the consul's question.

"My husband and I have visited your country. Nowhere have we found people we liked so well, or respected more for their efforts to overcome their difficulties. There is much we'd like to

learn about your people. Also, there's much we'd like to learn
from them. We want to go back and have our children know
them too."

Two months later the visas arrived with a package and a
note from the consul. "Dear Jill," it read. "Better take along
this bubble gum. It is the one strategic material America wants
that Indonesia lacks."

We left the *President Cleveland* in Hong Kong and flew to
Djakarta on a Dutch KLM plane. The craft was immaculate
and expertly handled. The stewardess was blond, pretty and
attentive. She showered the children with *hopjes* and treated
the rest of us to a splendid Dutch lunch. I relaxed in the air-
conditioned comfort and recalled my first visit to Djakarta, long
before the war. It was Batavia then, the proud capital of the
Netherlands East Indies. I remembered the strictly policed
traffic, the carefully manicured gardens, the deferential servants;
above all, the magnificent hospitality of the Hotel des Indes,
justly famed as the finest hostel in the East.

Fifteen years later, on my second visit, the city had changed
far more than in name. The decrepit buildings, the cracked
pavements, the jerry-built slums that had once been lovely parks
bore no resemblance to the fastidious colonial show place. The
once-orderly boulevards were a tangled snarl of battered cars
and bicycles. Homeless hordes of beggars and peddlers used the
sidewalks as spittoons. From the street, the Hotel des Indes
looked as gracious as ever, its dance floor and lounges gay with
pink-faced men and women quaffing Heineken's beer. Inside,
like all Djakarta, it was a shambles. Its disrepair, according to
rumor, was aided and abetted by its Dutch proprietors to shame
the Republic, and to make its most ardent well-wishers yearn

23

for the dear, dead Dutch days they, the proprietors, hoped were not beyond recall. For the children's sake, I prayed Djakarta had improved.

The courtesy with which we were ushered through customs deceived me into thinking that it had. Once outside the airport, my hopes sank. A Communist Party sign bade us welcome. Beside it stretched a huge banner emblazoned with one word, "Irian!" A ragged child tugged at my sleeve for alms. Crimson betel-nut juice gushed from a passerby's mouth and spattered Arthur's shoes. He insisted his feet were bleeding and hid his face in Eadie's skirt. The light of anticipation in Jill's eyes was washed away by tears.

Our travel agent finally appeared. A genial Dutchman, he explained that some stupid native clerk had mislaid my wire from Singapore advising his office of our arrival. He warned of trouble at the des Indes. It was packed to the rafters, he said, with Russians recently arrived to set up their new embassy and, he added, "sooner or later to take over the country." Our baggage aboard, he guided his car into the turbulent traffic streaming toward the city. Pedestrians and cyclists responded slowly to his horn. "Imbeciles," he swore. "The whole country is going to hell!"

Little outside the car window disputed him. We drove through a complex of shanty towns, gashed by canals used openly and indiscriminately for defecation and drinking. Buildings and walls wilted in the heat and bore, either stenciled or scrawled, the one word, "Irian!" The old Harmonie Club, once the temple of Dutch planters and traders, slid by, a sad, soiled shell. Beyond lay the des Indes's pretentious driveway.

A surly clerk registered us. A porter led us to two cells in a distant tier. A toilet and bath, shared by thirty guests, were a flight below. Their condition discouraged use except under du-

ress. Eadie bathed the children in a sink and put them to bed.
There were no mosquito bars. Bloody smears on the walls told
of nocturnal battles waged by previous tenants.

The heat discouraged sleep. Eadie and I went down to the
lounge for a drink. A trio of musicians pumped out fox trots
and waltzes. White and Chinese couples thronged the dance
floor. A familiar face rose from a distant table and beckoned.
It was an old Embassy friend, who invited us to join his party.
Consisting of the manager of an American oil field in Sumatra,
an English sugar refiner from Surabaja, a Dutch banker, and the
correspondent for a newspaper in New York, it was a gay group
until someone asked our mission in Indonesia. My answer induced a heavy silence, broken at last by the American oil man.
Sarcasm tinged his tone.

"My wife and I have been here nineteen years. All that time
we've had one house boy. We raised him like one of the family.
But when he goes back to his kampong, he might just as well be
off to the moon. As to what goes on inside his head, we haven't
a clue. If you ever discover what makes an Asian tick, do let me
know."

A sigh escaped the sugar man. "I felt sorry for the blokes
when I came out here. Raised the cane pickers' wages the first
chance I could. Next day no one showed for work. We lost a
lot of sugar. Company asks us to treat them like human beings
—better conditions, inducements, that sort of thing. Nothing
works the way it does with normal people. I've given up trying
to figure the devils out."

My Embassy friend shook his head sadly. "Frankly, we've
never tried to understand the rank and file of Indonesians. We
deal exclusively with the big wheels and count on them to reach
the masses. Once, when the politicians and the people were
united by the urge for freedom, the method worked. Today,

25

there's no longer one ideal to bind the high and low together. The leaders and intellectuals have lost contact with the masses. And so have we."

The Dutch banker laughed. "You Americans amuse me. You have your Negroes. You treat them like the children God meant them to be. Yet you come here and turn these savages' heads by your efforts to 'understand' them. You might just as well try to understand the monkeys in the zoo."

The correspondent was reminded of a story. "Doubtless you've seen the signs all over the city. Irian is the local name for Dutch New Guinea. Sukarno has sworn to take it from the Dutch and is doing all he can to arouse the people. Anyway, an American like yourself arrived to study the average Indonesian. He wondered how much the Irian issue really meant to the masses. To find out he called his cook. 'Tell me, Koki, what is Irian?' After long thought she said she didn't know but would inquire in her kampong. Next morning she reported, 'Irian is the name of President Sukarno's sister. The Dutch kidnaped her, raped her and refused to let her go. We cannot allow the Dutch to treat the President's sister so cruelly. It's Irian or war!'"

The correspondent polished off his beer. "I'd give a lot to know if that story is apocryphal. Are Asia's masses really that dumb, or are they smarter than some of us think? Asia's fate—and ours too—depends on the answer."

Next morning the official in the Ministry of Information mulled over my request for advice on where to work.

"Indonesia," he said at last, in excellent English, "is big. It has two hundred ethnic groups and forty languages. You couldn't possibly know them all. But more than half of our eighty million people live here in Java. In central Java our culture is purest, yet it is adapting daily to changing times. My suggestion is, settle somewhere around here." His finger circled the map around Surakarta. "Work out into the surrounding villages. Then follow some of the transmigrants from the area to Sumatra, where they are carving new lives in the jungle. That way you can encompass the past, present and future of our country.

"Surakarta," he continued, "is the center of the universe. A tower has stood there for centuries to mark the spot on which the world revolves. Recently it burned down. Next day the monsoons broke early. Spirits, weeping at the tower's loss, caused the rain. The city has some of our finest theaters and music, and just the right combination of farming and light industry to give you insight into our economic problems. Another thing, Surakarta's women are famed for their beauty and passion."

I explained that my wife and children would be with me. "In that case," said the official, "housing will be a consideration. Every inch is occupied, but it happens that the palace of one of the local princes has been converted into a small hostel. It is our way of forcing our aristocrats to invest their gold in useful projects. It stands close to the center of town, right across from the Sriwedari, a pleasure park where wajang, or shadow plays, are performed. To know our people, you must know our wajang. In Surakarta you will eat wajang, drink wajang, sleep wajang. It goes on night and day."

The official's expression suddenly turned serious. "A word of warning," he said. "Do not become involved in local politics. Throughout its history, the town has been a political hotbed. It all began long ago when one of its rulers, the Susuhunan of Kartasura, got into an argument with the Chinese over a matter

27

of the heart. The Chinese wanted him to marry one of their princesses. His desire lay elsewhere. Fighting destroyed much of the city. Then the Dutch intervened and burned down what was left. The Susuhunan, anxious to escape the scene of so much trouble, rebuilt his palace a short distance away. To reverse his fortunes, he reversed the name of his former capital, Kartasura, and called his new home Surakarta.

"It is our custom," the official explained, "to change our names when we are unlucky. But in this instance, the change did not help. The Dutch grew jealous of the Susuhunan's popularity and set up a competing prince, Mangkunegoro. Ever since, Surakarta's loyalties have been split between the rival houses. During the recent fighting, much of it centering around the city, neither prince defended the revolution and, as a result, both forfeited their popularity and power. They still meddle in cultural matters, but it will do you no good to get mixed up with them. Just keep your heart and mind as open as your eyes and ears, and Surakarta will tell you everything you want to know about us."

Eadie and I talked it over. Despite the beauty and passion of its women, the Center of the Universe, she agreed, sounded perfect for our purpose.

THREE

The Frogs under
the Coconut Shell

THE PLANE circled the flats around Djakarta and pointed inland toward the mountains, some of them rice-terraced almost to their summits, verdant, the water in the paddies shimmering in the sunshine. The central range mastered after an hour's flight, the southern coast came into view. We descended to Maguwo airport, a brown speck on the green carpet of central Java. Switching to a car, we sped along a good highway, past fields of rice, sugar, cassava and corn. In the distance smoked Merapi volcano, fertilizing the land with its ash. Here and there rose the ruins of lacy Hindu temples, the soil about them cultivated to their crumbling foundations by farmers pushing plows almost as old as the mossy stones. Joy returned to the children's faces and to Eadie's heart and mine. This was Java, here was the land, these were the people we had come so far to know.

Beside the Solo River, Java's largest and loveliest, sprawled the city. Our driver said people called the city Solo too. We entered between two monumental pillars and drove down the main street, named the Slamet Rijadi after a gallant revolutionary fighter, and bordered by Dutch bungalows converted into government offices, barracks and schools. A railroad shared the street with horse-drawn surreys, tricycle taxis called *betchas*, barefoot pedestrians and herds of goats and geese. Venders of food, toys, eyeglasses, magic potions, haircuts and horoscopes squatted along the footpath. Two movie theaters dominated the main intersection, their flamboyant billboards advertising an American gangland thriller and a propaganda film from Peiping. Run-down and architecturally undistinguished, Solo nevertheless looked alive and gay; the only note of sorrow was cast by the rubble of buildings wrecked during the revolution.

The Prince's palace, where we were to live, faced the Slamet Rijadi. It consisted of a rather elegant central building bordered on three sides by connecting cottages, each with its own garden and porch. Outside it resembled a Miami motel, but the reception hall and dining room, with eight carved pillars supporting an intricately sculptured ceiling, and our bathroom, with its hip-high tub of cool water, were Javanese. We introduced Jill and Arthur to their first Indonesian bath, filling a gourd with water and splashing them thoroughly. They loved not having to worry about wet floors and walls, and we all emerged clean, happy and hungry.

In the dining room an old man, barefoot and garbed in a bright sarong, set before us bowls of rice, curried vegetables, and bananas fried in coconut oil. The children sampled the fare and almost retched. From an adjoining table a tow-headed family wafted us sympathetic smiles. The man came over and introduced himself as Dr. Heintz. He was a boyish, crew-cropped Wehrmacht veteran from Leipzig who, to escape the Communists, had wangled a three-year contract with a local hospital. His wife, Helena, plumply pretty, had eyebrows which con-

30

veyed her emotions better than did her halting English. At the moment their sharp angle expressed hunger. With their two boys, about Jill's and Arthur's ages, the Heintzes comprised Solo's entire foreign population. Our arrival swelled it to eight.

Dr. Heintz said the absentee Prince's hospitality made few concessions to Western palates and local shops stocked little with which to augment the royal table. Until recently there had been bread of sorts, but government restrictions on flour imports had cut off this staple from their diet. Helena said the only escape from starvation was the Malang, a Chinese restaurant where, several evenings a week, they gorged on prawns, pigeon and other delicatessen. The Malang was to see us often. That evening, however, Jill and Arthur met hunger for the first time. It was to become a familiar companion in the months ahead.

I lost no time, next morning, getting down to work. My greatest need was an interpreter. From Heintz and others I learned of a man who spoke low, middle and high Javanese and English. Son of a hadji—one who had made the pilgrimage to Mecca—and himself a good Moslem, he had studied during Dutch times in a Catholic school, had edited the local newspaper, and now served as agent for the Garuda airways, an undemanding job. His name was Samiek, meaning breast-sucker.

Samiek proved to be a tawny Falstaff. From his round waist up, he wore Western clothes except for the black velvet cap that is Indonesia's national headgear. His lower extremities were swathed in a flowered sarong. His dark eyes were brightly shrewd, his voice loud, his laugh hearty. I liked him on sight and came abruptly to the point of my business. Starting with the birth of a baby, I told him, I wanted to witness everything that happened to an infant, a child, an adult throughout an entire life cycle. I wanted to visit schools, mosques, clubs, labor unions, theaters and family celebrations. I wanted to talk with farmers, workers, students, teachers, merchants and civil servants. Everything that happened to people, I said, was important, from the lullaby that mothers sang to their babies, to the services beside the grave. I asked Samiek to tell me frankly if he thought this could be done.

"Ten Indian boats come into the harbor," said Samiek cryptically, "but the dog's tail stays between his legs. Some people shy away from what is strange. If you are one who will condemn or mock our ways, you will learn nothing."

I assured him I was without prejudice, fully aware that though his people's customs might differ from mine they deserved as much respect.

"My people," said Samiek, "are like frogs under a coconut shell. Since the shell is all they have known, they think it is the universe. And so, since all the white men they have known have been Dutchmen, *belandas,* you will be a *belanda* too. They will fear you like a tiger that hides its claws. It will take time before they will speak frankly in your presence."

"Where I live," I said, "people also believe in knowing a man's character before they trust him. Anyway, let us try. I will need all of your time for many months. We must arrange a schedule. We must settle the matter of your pay."

Samiek rose. "A sarong," he said, "is used as a protection against nettles. Money is used as protection against shame. I have another engagement. Please excuse me."

Samiek's addiction to proverbs added spice to his speech, but left me uncertain of his meaning. His parting words made me suspect that my brusque reference to time schedules and payment had offended him. When days passed and he did not return, I was sure. Idleness was irksome and, on my own, I started to explore the city. Following the *rijadi,* I strolled past a stone prison and the post office to the Susuhunan's palace, fronting on a broad, dusty square shaded by holy trees and dominated by two medieval cannon converted into shrines. The labyrinth of narrow streets surrounding the square hid many mosques, a Chinese temple, the vegetable, meat and bird markets, the pawnshops and innumerable stores. From the poorly paved streets grassy lanes wandered off into the kampongs where dwelt the majority of Solo's three hundred thousand citizens. Each a little ward of about a hundred families, they seemed much like the villages on the road from Maguwo, pressed tightly together. Huts of split-bamboo matting stood in the shade of banana and palm trees, each on its own brown patch of beaten earth fringed with fruit-bearing bushes, and each filled with children and chickens. The air was pungent with the sweet smell of clove tobacco and the heavier smoke of charcoal fires oozing from the windowless walls. Narrow paths, bordered by open sewers, led to other kampongs, spaced farther and farther apart as they ranged outward from the heart of the city until, imperceptibly, town and country merged.

In one of these kampongs I passed a meat vender's stall and watched while he spitted tidbits of goatflesh on bamboo sticks, dipped them in hot sauces, and roasted a half-dozen sticks at a time over hot coals. Famished, I squatted between a *betcha* driver and a farmer laden with chicken-filled baskets for the market. The vender gave the sticks a final twirl and offered them to me. I pointed to my neighbors. The farmer accepted them and smiled. The *betcha* boy said, *"Belanda."* I shook my head and said "American." He shrugged. In the dirt I sketched the stars and stripes. Both men looked and repeated, *"Belanda."*

My meat was ready and I dug my teeth into the hot morsels. The others watched and laughed. The *betcha* boy said, *"Tidah belanda."* Another man stooped beside us. It was Samiek. "They

33

say you are not a Dutchman," he said. "You eat *sate* just like they do. They ask which you like best, heart, liver or flesh?" I said I liked them all. *"Bagus,"* they said, "good!" We all shared another round of *sate* with Samiek. Then, rubbing the grease off our fingers in the grass, we rose and shook hands. Samiek walked home with me.

"A torch," he said, "is useless to a blind man. I shall hold up the light. Whether or not you see is up to you. Soon a neighbor's wife in my kampong will give birth. You cannot use a rice thresher to pull a thorn. You cannot buy your way to the house of my neighbor with money. But we Javanese like to have pictures of ourselves, our wives, our children. Perhaps, if you will present him with pictures of the birthday celebration, you will be welcome."

Never, thereafter, did I try to pin down Samiek to work schedules and rates of pay. Nor, to any Indonesians, did I ever again mention money. Not that such practical matters were overlooked. It was just that there was a right way and there was a wrong way to go about them.

The dirt floor of Samiek's neighbor's house was covered with a reed mat, set with banana leaves piled with rice and the meat, offal and eye of a buffalo. Male relatives and friends sat cross-legged along the walls. A *modin*—a layman learned in the Koran—mumbled a prayer. Behind a bamboo partition, women clustered about the mother-to-be, a child in her early teens named Rahaju. She lay upon newspapers spread over the earth. A *dukun,* or witch doctor, knelt beside her. As the rhythm of labor began, the *dukun* poured water into a bowl and added turmeric. The water turned yellow and she dropped in a brightly polished coin. Samiek explained that the "gold water" was a disinfectant and astringent for mother and child. The coin betokened wealth.

Djogo, the young husband, a sandal cobbler by trade, was enthralled by my camera. When the natal moment approached, he insisted that I photograph the entrance of his first-born into the world. He sat on the floor and cradled Rahaju's head in his arms. The *dukun* gently pressed the girl's abdomen and arranged a sarong around her outspread limbs. She prayed to the good and evil spirits which, Samiek said, invade houses at this critical time. Djogo began to blow on Rahaju's head, gently at first, harder as the spasms quickened. The *dukun* crooned, "Give it to me, mother. Come out, baby. Come out quickly, little one. Bring your brother, the afterbirth, with you. The gold water is ready to wash you."

The girl responded silently to the *dukun*'s coaching. "Rest now. Breathe easily. Now push hard and bite your hair. Allah be praised! It is coming! Here it is! Give thanks to Allah! It is a boy!"

The *dukun* rubbed the umbilical cord, then cut it with the sharp edge of a piece of bamboo. Blood was rubbed on the infant's lips "to keep them always red." The *dukun* dipped the baby, a lusty six-pounder, in the gold water, wrapped it in a clean cloth, and placed it by the mother. Fully conscious, Rahaju smiled down upon it through happy tears.

Djogo held a clay pot to catch the afterbirth. Rice, salt, flowers and perfume were added, followed by a coin, a pencil, a sheet of paper with Arabic characters. Samiek whispered that the placenta was the baby's younger brother who would watch after his well-being from the spirit world. The coin invited wealth, the pencil knowledge; the Arabic characters signified ability to read the Koran. We followed Djogo, who carried the

35

pot in one hand, an umbrella in the other, to a hole dug beside the door. There he buried it and reverently covered the grave with flowers.

Within the house, the sarong was stripped off Rahaju, never to be used again except to cover the child in times of illness. The *modin* struck three sharp blows near the infant's head, to make sure it would not grow up to be nervous or lacking in poise. Then he whispered into his left ear: "God the Almighty, I swear there is no other God than Allah. I testify that Mohammed is His messenger. Come, we shall pray. Praying is more important than sleeping. Allah the Almighty, we beg good fortune. There is no other God than Allah."

The guests divided the food, wrapped their portions into banana-leaf parcels and, wishing Djogo well, left for their homes. Each reminded Samiek not to forget their pictures and invited me and my camera to be present at events impending in their families.

I was elated at the success of Samiek's stratagem, but also disturbed. I felt that my presence during the more intimate moments of Rahaju's childbirth had been an intrusion. Moreover, the camera had taken so much of my time that my notes had suffered. It seemed to me we needed a photographer on our team. Samiek produced a gaunt, raffish character named Bambang. From a Dutch news photographer to whom he had apprenticed himself, Bambang had acquired not only mastery of the lens, but other tricks as well. He handled his Speed Graphic like a pistol, bullied his subjects unmercifully, and behaved generally in the exaggerated manner Hollywood deems appropriate to his trade. Samiek, of course, had a proverb to fit him:

"If the teacher urinates while walking, the pupil urinates while he runs."

Between them, Samiek and Bambang could transform my most improbable requests into action. They knew everything happening within a ten-mile radius of the city. Here a girl was being "circumcised." There a thief was being tried. In a distant kampong, a man was divorcing his wife. In another, a farmers' co-operative was meeting, or the Communists were staging a rally. None of these events was announced in my daily newspaper. No telephones connected Solo with these obscure villages. The pair clearly had sources of information and means of communication of their own. I counted on time to solve these and other mysteries that baffled Eadie and me.

One of the oddest of these was Samiek's habit of never being content with a gift. When Eadie learned that he was married, she gave him a small brooch for his wife. He astonished her by asking whether she had any others. She hadn't, and Samiek looked pained. On another occasion, when I bought flowers for Eadie, I presented Samiek with an identical bouquet to take home. He stared at it almost in dismay, as though it were in some respect deficient. Whatever we gave him, we invariably were left with the feeling that he was reproachful rather than grateful. In a more mercenary man, such behavior would have been less strange. It didn't fit Samiek.

Neither did his moodiness on Fridays. A garrulous, laughter-loving companion throughout the week, on this one day he was always glum and fidgety. On Fridays, too, Bambang's hand shook and his pictures came out blurred. Neither would volunteer an explanation.

Of all Samiek's idiosyncrasies, the one that puzzled us most was his behavior at mealtimes. Never a punctual man—"In

37

Indonesia," he'd say, "even time is made of rubber"—he always displayed deep anxiety about the hour at noon and sundown. Murmuring that his wife was waiting, he would hastily leave. Eadie and I could understand his hunger, which we shared, but never the fact that he always took off in a different direction. We became more and more curious about Mrs. Samiek.

Bambang was also married but he flirted atrociously with every pretty girl he met, apparently with great success. He enjoyed being teased about his conquests, laughing, looking knowingly at Samiek and saying nothing. We added this to our growing list of enigmas.

Only once did we quarrel. I wanted complete photographic coverage of a wajang performance at the Sriwedari. The mayor of Solo, in charge of such matters, granted permission with reluctance. We laid careful plans to exploit our opportunity. Samiek would translate the dialogue word by word. Bambang would move about below the stage, keeping one eye on the action, the other on me. Whenever I wanted a picture, I'd raise my hand. It was a foolproof arrangement except that, in the middle of the last act, Bambang ran out of flashbulbs.

Samiek quipped that Bambang's arms were too short to embrace the mountain. Bambang shrugged the matter off. I scolded them both for being so irresponsible and wasting the long evening's work. When my tirade ended, Samiek stood up. "When we do well, we smell like flowers. When we fail, we smell like excrement. When your nose decides how we really smell, let us know."

Shame overcame me when the mayor sent a note saying the play would be rescheduled so that his friend Bambang could photograph the final act. I searched all over town for the pair.

"Forgive me," I said. "You are flowers, now and forever."

Samiek said, "Americans can solve all life's secrets, but they do not know that in a thousand years nothing matters." Then they laughed. Thereafter, I kept a tight reign on my temper.

As I had hoped, time and propinquity cleared up some of the mystery cloaking Samiek and Bambang. Blue Fridays, for instance. It turned out that Solo folk believe that evil spirits called *demits* attack people in bed on Thursday nights. Everyone visited or walked the streets until dawn, making up the lost sleep on Friday, the Moslem Sabbath. Only Samiek and Bambang, trying to appease both the *demits* and me, suffered. As much for my sake as theirs, I changed our day of rest to Friday.

Bambang's sexual ardor turned out to be a matter of politics rather than glands. "For as long as anyone can remember," he finally admitted, "every Indonesian learned that the Dutchman was a better man than he—in the Army, the schools, the civil service. There was only one way and place that we could prove we were better than the *belandas*. That was in bed. When you tease me about my passion, I laugh. I am not laughing at your joke, but at the Dutchmen."

None of these oddities struck me as anything more than amusing until, one day, an Englishman arrived in Solo. Smythe was with a large European tobacco concern which manufactured cigarettes for the Indonesian market. When imports were cut off, the local tobacco had become important. Smythe, convinced that Java's soil would produce fine Kentucky tobacco, had given seedlings free to any farmers who would take them. He had also taught them the best cultivation and fire-curing techniques. A fine crop had resulted. Now he was going out to pay the growers a surprise visit and look into the marketing. I accepted his invitation to go along. It seemed a rare chance to see foreign enterprise at its most enlightened.

39

It turned out at the first village that our arrival was expected. About twenty farmers were waiting, the local Communist leader at their head. Their manner was sullen, and I suddenly remembered it was Friday. The Communist spokesman, a lean, intense man, spurned Smythe's hand and announced that the company was cheating the farmers. Smythe calmly asked how.

"The company's prices are too low," said the other, and the farmers growled agreement. Smythe drew a copy of a contract from his brief case and began to read its terms relative to prices.

A farmer interrupted. "We cannot read your contract. It is men we trust, not written words. You promised us a higher price for Kentucky than for our *krossok* tobacco. Instead, we are getting less."

Smythe's face reddened. "Naturally," he said. "We paid high prices early in the harvest. Now with so much Kentucky on the market, prices are bound to be lower. That's the law of supply and demand."

The Communist said, "We understand but one law, Allah's." Smythe's temper frayed. "How dare you, a Bolshevik, talk about Allah!" He waved the contract in front of the farmers' faces. "This is the tobacco code! This is what we promised! This is what we pay!"

A farmer answered. "This is our country. We have our own code. You gave us the seedlings to place us in your debt. You promised many things but hid your true meaning in printed words we cannot read. Now, instead of payment, we get excuses. This is what comes of trusting a *belanda*."

Back in the car, Smythe mopped his forehead. "Bloody silly of me to lose my temper. How can you do business with people like that?"

I admitted I didn't know and told him of my own errors in dealing with Samiek and Bambang. "Maybe," I said, "we ought to know more about their outlook on business, their ethics, their terms."

Smythe seemed dubious. "But I say," he exclaimed, "I'd like to meet your Samiek. Maybe he can tell me how the beggars knew I was coming!"

Samiek was nowhere about. Eadie said that though it was Friday he had worked with her on newspaper translations all afternoon. Then, suddenly uneasy, he had left just before supper.

I slept fitfully that night, disturbed by the day's misadventure. I had seen the heavy Kentucky bursting from the soil, and the scrawny patches of native *krossok*. Smythe deserved credit for every leaf. What a paradox that the Communist should be the farmers' champion, and Smythe be cast as their foe. I measured the gulf of ignorance that divided me from these people—even from Samiek, whom I should certainly know by this time. Why, I wondered, was Samiek so disturbed whenever he left us? Where did he go? Who was the mysterious Mrs. Samiek? Why were our gifts never enough?

The answers came months later.

"As a Moslem," Samiek said, "I am allowed four wives. I have taken full advantage of my privilege. But each is jealous of the others, and I keep them far apart, in different kampongs. Allah help me if I forget with which woman I am to share a meal or bed. Their tongues have no bones. Should one receive a gift, the others know of it before it is out of my hand. Women!" He spat out the word as though it were bitter. "They are blind to an elephant on their eyelids. But a louse they can observe on the other side of the sea!"

FOUR

The Day Jill Danced in the Rain

SHORTLY AFTER our arrival in Solo, Jill rose early one morning and bicycled down to the narrow canal separating our garden from the neighboring kampong. Tending a goose beside the water was a girl of her age, her slim body sheathed in a length of tattered batik. The children stared shyly at each other. Then the Javanese girl touched the bicycle and said, *"Baik."* Jill pointed at the bird and said, "Goose." The other nodded happily. A few minutes later, Jill was at our door with her new friend.

"Mommy," she cried, "Seneng and I talk the same language! And she's given me her goose!"

Eadie had a little trouble explaining that *baik* and *bagus* were Malay words, both meaning good, and that their resemblance to bike and goose was a coincidence. She had even greater difficulty separating Jill from the goose. She finally succeeded in returning the pet, but she could not shake Jill's conviction that she and Seneng were linked by a bond of mutual understanding. Nor could she convince her that it was wrong to accept gifts from someone so poor. Indeed, upon two stubbornly held beliefs—that she and the Javanese were pretty much the same kind of people, and that there was nothing wrong in taking from them all she could get—Jill proceeded to build solid friendships with the kampong youngsters.

We unashamedly eavesdropped on her talks with the goose-girl. With Samiek's help, these conversations came to cover a wide area of topics. Seneng's name was among the first.

"It's so pretty," said Jill. "Who are you named after?"

"No one," said Seneng. "My name means 'happy.' I used to be called Samadi until I got sick. Samadi means 'thoughtful.' The *dukun* said that since I wasn't a thoughtful person the name was making me sick. So they called me 'Happy' instead. Right away I felt better. All the children in the kampong have names that fit them. If they don't, they die."

Jill insisted neither that Seneng's illness was due to bacteria nor that her recovery resulted from antibodies built up in her blood. She accepted the Javanese way as normal and right. It never became an issue—a conscious or hidden difference from which might be inferred the superiority of one system over the other. On the contrary, evidence that Seneng's world was largely one of supersitition didn't faze Jill in the least. She simply added belief in the occult to her belief in science, feeling herself enriched rather than demeaned by the addition.

Since Jill was so obviously healthy, Seneng decided her name must be right. Chubby Arthur, however, was nicknamed Semar. The name was pinned on him after our first attendance at a wajang, a shadow play based on a tale from the Hindu Rama-yana. The play dealt with war between two mythical kingdoms, one led by five noble brothers, the other ruled by an evil minis-ter. A note of humor was supplied by the fat, foolish servant of the five princes, a clown named Semar. Arthur's paunch unmis-

takably resembled Semar's. He wept at being named after a
clown. He wanted to be called Arjuna, bravest of the princes—
until Seneng sat him on her lap and explained:

"Semar stands for the people." (This was how Samiek passed
on Seneng's words.) "He seems stupid, but actually he is the
wisest of all. The people, too, may seem like dumb servants of
their rulers, but they have both the wisdom and the power.
Now, aren't you happy to be called Semar?"

Arthur agreed and thereafter bore his nickname proudly.
Whether he really grasped the meaning of Seneng's words was
doubtful, but Jill, through the explanation of this Asian girl her
own age, began to understand subtle political concepts which
never, at home, had been clear. That the wisdom of the masses
surpassed any individual's, that rulers were helpless without the
people's support—ideas like these were suddenly illuminated
by a symbol like Semar. Nor had pat phrases like "the dignity
of the common man" or "the sanctity of the human personality"
had much meaning until, one day, she returned from Seneng's
house, both elated and disturbed by what she had seen.

"Seneng's father," she said, "was playing with Widodo, the
baby. It was all fun until Widodo pulled his hair. The father
flicked his ear until he cried. Seneng was so scared, she could
hardly tell me what was wrong. 'He touched my father's head,'
was all she'd say. Later she explained that God lives inside the
human head. Every child is taught never to touch his father's
head. I felt sorry for little Widodo," Jill concluded, "but isn't
it wonderful to know that God lives inside human beings?"

Reminded of her own Sunday-school teaching, Jill nodded.
"Sure," she said, "we all believe the same thing. But golly, to
these people it's so *important!*"

Javanese discipline in general impressed Jill deeply. She was
fascinated by the five rules on which Seneng was raised. Each

44

rule was embodied in a Javanese word beginning with M: *Main*
—do not gamble. *Madon*—do not lust. *Madat*—do not smoke
opium. *Maling*—do not steal. *Minum*—do not get drunk. That
Seneng had to be warned against sins of such caliber gave her
added stature in the eyes of Jill, brought up on the milder
Golden Rule.

Seneng, to our knowledge, never violated any of the "Five
Ms." For her lesser infractions, her mother flicked her ear, more
hurtful to her pride than to her lobe. Spankings and other
forms of bodily punishment, visited upon a smaller person by
a larger one, were rare. A perceptible change overtook Jill's
own behavior toward her smaller brother. Where once she had
not hesitated to bind him to her will by superior force, now she
sought to win him with sweet talk. An earlier tendency to glory
in her size, and to boast about how big everything was at home,
shifted to the reverse, an emphasis on the diminutive—such as
how small was the town we came from, and how tiny our house.

The reason turned out to be a mouse deer named Kantjil, the
wee hero of all Javanese children. Jill never tired of listening
to tales about Kantjil, all of which stressed the same moral: By
wit and cunning, little Kantjil mastered his bigger, stronger
foes. Her favorite was one about Kantjil and the elephant. The
mouse deer had fallen into a dry well and had almost given up
hope of getting out when along came the elephant. "What are
you doing down there, Kantjil?" he asked. "Look up," said
Kantjil. "Can't you see those clouds? The heavens are about to
fall down, and I've found the safest place to hide." Frightened,
the elephant jumped into the hole. "Well," said Kantjil, "I'd
better take a closer look at the clouds and see whether the
heavens will fall now or later. Just lift me gently to your
back." It was just a short jump from the elephant's back to the

ground, and safety. Kantjil scampered off, delighted at having outwitted the big, stupid elephant.

Reliance on wit to overcome size also featured the children's games. To decide who would start a game, they "chose" with their fingers. The thumb was the elephant, the index finger a man, the pinky an ant. Thumb won over index finger because an elephant can kill a man. But pinky won over thumb, because an ant can crawl inside an elephant's brain and kill him. Every boy learned how a blow to vital nerve centers, coupled with skill in leverage, could overcome a larger adversary. This science, known as *pentjak,* turned size into a disadvantage. As Seneng pointed out, "How else do you suppose a small people like us overthrew the Dutch?"

Stimulated by this novel theory, Jill asked what, in turn, could overcome the Javanese? Seneng replied by teaching Jill the Javanese alphabet. Each written letter, she explained, must be pronounced unless a little mark, resembling an *L,* was placed beneath it. "The *L* is like a human lap. To quiet a baby, you sit it on your lap. To silence a letter, you sit it on this 'lap.' Our teacher says that the only way a Javanese can be silenced is to 'sit us on a lap.' We can be overcome by kindness, never by size and force."

Seneng then coupled every two letters of the alphabet to form words, which formed a little poem.

> *There were two messengers.*
> *They were fighting.*
> *They were equally strong.*
> *They killed each other.*

"This poem," she said, "is about a rajah who decided to visit another land. Before leaving, he handed his sword to one of his servants. 'Keep it and give it into no other hand than mine,' he said. Later, the Rajah needed his sword and sent a second servant to get it. Both men were faithful to the Rajah's commands. They fought and killed each other. Our teacher says the story means that there are two great nations in the world. Each claims that its own message is the only true one. They fight, and in the end both will die. Our teacher says it is important for us to have our own message of truth, and not to get mixed up in the wars of the big nations."

Cold war, neutralism, propaganda lay outside Jill's ken. But one day she said, "I'd like to write a book about America that tells how small and clever we are. Then the people here would know we are more like Kantjil, the way they are, instead of a bunch of stupid elephants crashing through the world."

The only American publication Jill had, aside from her textbooks, was her Girl Scout Manual. Scouting is a popular institution in Indonesia. An avid Brownie, Jill threw herself joyfully into the marches, drills and other activities of the kampong's troop, closely paralleling her own unit's at home. Believing that the others would be interested in her manual, she took it with her to a meeting. It turned out that they had already seen it.

"We received many copies as gifts from America," the leader explained. "But after seeing what was in them, we threw them away. To a Moslem it is shameful to name oneself after beavers, wolves and bears, and to copy their ways. Our scouting is based on the human family. That is why I am not a scoutmaster. We have had enough of masters in Indonesia. I am an *ibunda,* a parent, to my patrol. I do not teach the manual's code of the jungle. Instead, I teach the code of the wajang princes, which is noble, and close to God."

Jill was mad clear through when she reported the incident. "Gee," she said, "they *need* those manuals. Imagine throwing

47

them away for a little thing like that!" Then she held her head as though it ached with remorse, or wisdom. "But I guess, maybe, it isn't such a *little* thing to them. Maybe whoever sent that book should have *known* about Moslems!"

Jill learned about Islam in the madrasah, or religious school, that Seneng attended. Far from being excluded as an infidel, she was welcomed as an honored guest. She discovered the religious basis of the scouts' aversion to animals, for the Koran seemed especially strict about avoiding the slobbering of dogs and contact with animals related to them. Religion seemed to be largely a set of rules governing diet and cleanliness; as for ethics, these derived mainly from tales drawn from the life of Mohammed. She learned how good the Prophet had been to his mother, how he respected his elders, how he honored the dead.

None of this disturbed her until, one day, the teacher talked about tolerance. "Mohammed," he said, "had a visitor from Medina, a Christian. Mohammed gave him food and shelter and, on Sunday, permitted him to pray in a mosque in the Christian way. Mohammed's example taught the Christian the truth—that there is but one God. He has no son. He has no mother. He has but one Prophet. And so the Christian became a Moslem and found the way to God."

For several days after hearing this story, Jill seemed estranged from her friends. Fearing that the contradiction of her own teaching might have created a crisis in faith, Eadie asked whether she could help to resolve the questions or doubts that were troubling her. "Oh, no," she said, "it isn't that at all. It's just that for the first time in my life I had the feeling that someone felt *sorry* for me. The minute I thought the other kids felt better than me, I stopped liking them. It's awful, Mommy, to be looked down on. But I'm getting over it. We all *do* believe in God, and I guess that's what really matters. All I hope is that we don't ever give them the feeling we look down on *them!"*

Jill passed through another crisis in public school. Instead of Washington and Lincoln, pictures of strange heroes adorned the classroom walls—Erlangga, Kertanagara, Diponegoro— venerated not alone because they had liberated and unified their country, but because, like Kantjil, they had won their battles with brain, not might. The parallel between Indonesia's revolution and America's did not escape her. She searched, in both her American and her Indonesian textbooks, for passages that stressed this identity. In the one she found nothing on Indonesia. In the other, she discovered what Indonesians learn about the United States:

The name America reminds people of different things. Some remember the skyscrapers, others think of moving pictures, or of motorcars and planes. But you must not imagine every American lives in a skyscraper or works in a motorcar factory, or in the film industry. In America, many people work and live under the ground. . . . In the U.S.A. (don't be alarmed) there are about 30 million motorcars—we can say that each family has at least one car. In the factories, each worker has one task. One puts on wheels, the other changes screws, another keeps records. You know, it would make us weary, wouldn't it? How different, for instance, from a silver worker in Indonesia. You must admit that our way gives us more satisfaction. "Time is money" is the American maxim.

One morning I sat in on one of Jill's classes. In my honor, the teacher conducted a quiz on America. It was the sixth grade, the children ranging in age from ten to twelve.

"Who is the President of the United States?"

"Dwiad Eisen Hower."

"Where does he live?"

"In a white building."

"What does America produce?"

"Machinery and guns."

"Are there any Indonesians in America?"

"Yes, they are learning to be Air Force pilots in California."

"What else happens in California?"

"Marilyn Monroe."

"Would you like to visit America?"

Most of the children said yes, for different reasons: "Because America is where the movies come from." "Because everyone in America is rich." "Because I want to see the skyscrapers."

A few said no— "Because America is full of kissing and killing." "Because America hates colored people like us." "Because if I went to America, they'd arrest me and make me pick cotton."

Jill regained her sense of balance sooner than I. "Gosh," she said, "if you asked the kids in my class at home about Indonesia, they wouldn't even know what you meant." At the same time, she began a campaign of counterpropaganda to sell America to her schoolmates. It was her one great failure. Whether because it violated their Kantjil philosophy, or because Indonesians loathe immodesty, the children interpreted the mildest self-praise as bombast. To make matters worse, Jill fell into the trap that invites all propagandists—exaggeration.

During one period when a rash of movies dramatizing juvenile delinquency broke out in Solo's theaters, she was taunted about America's children preferring gangs to school. Jill protested hotly. "American kids *love* school! My school is so crowded, the kids fall out of the windows!" For weeks, she was asked whether these falls killed or injured many children. Jill finally learned to keep her mouth shut. Her silence was a signal to her closer friends to do battle for her, and for America. Somehow, coming from them, praise of America was more acceptable to the others.

We feared that Jill was making an even more serious error in failing to curb her acquisitiveness. Whatever she saw, she admired and wanted. She came home from the kampongs loaded with gifts. We scolded her for taking so much and giving so little. "But they love to give me things," she insisted. "They're happy when I like them."

We returned most of the jewelry and toys but hadn't the heart to deprive her of the dancing costume Seneng's father had given her. For Jill had become entranced with the *srimpi* dance of Java. From Seneng's father, each afternoon after his work in the batik factory was finished, she learned its difficult discipline of mind and body. For a while we felt that this enthusiasm, like so many others before it, would pass. Instead, it mounted, and with it her demands on Seneng's father's time. I finally decided to make some arrangement with him.

I started for his home under lowering skies, for the monsoons had broken. Soon rain was falling in torrents, the day turned black, and our path became a rushing stream. None of this prepared me for the spectacle that greeted me in the kampong. Water lay a foot deep in the courtyard and covered the floors of the house. Rain gushed through loose tiles in the roof. Oblivious, the man and the child were dancing together.

"Now kneel, *genduk*," he said. "Ask the earth for strength, for the earth gives you power. Raise your hands before your face. Honor God, and honor yourself as a human being. Bring together the tips of your fingers. The thumb is God, the little finger is the people. There can be harmony only when God and the people meet."

Crouching along the walls, the kampong folk watched with

shining eyes. I joined them, and when the lesson was over I left without making any arrangement with Seneng's father.

Jill had her tenth birthday party in Solo. All the kampong children came with gifts and little speeches. They were simple and charming, but the one that moved us most was Seneng's.

"When we met," was its gist, "Jill did not draw away. We talked and discovered we were equal—equal in our hunger for the other, and equal in ignorance of each other. She taught me and I taught her, as equals. She did not laugh at our ways, and I did not laugh at hers. Instead, Jill liked our ways and asked us for many things. First, she asked for my goose. Next, she asked for our language. Then she asked for our stories, our songs, our dance. We gave them to her proudly. We entrust them to her because she loves them. She proved her love and won our love, the day Jill danced in the rain."

These modern Indonesian girls learning midwifery from charts will help to make up for the crucial lack of doctors and will be a scientific advance over the *dukun,* or witch doctor, shown here with her herbal remedies.

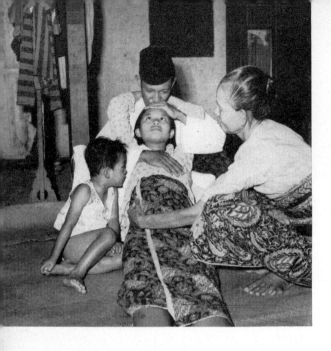

It is not unusual for children to attend births. Here Rahaju is in labor. Below, her husband takes the baby's
"younger brother," the placenta, out to bury it at the door.

Rahaju nurses her baby, Sulisto, who brings his own quantity of luck into the world, increasing the family's treasure.

On his first birthday a child may climb a banana ladder (foreground, left) leading to happiness and receive gifts like this rocket-firing jeep.

An airplane and a wajang puppet symbolize the present con-
flict of Indonesia's future and past. Below, the children of
Solo play a game in which a doll dances magically under a
full moon.

Almost every village now boasts an elementary school, where study includes not only reading and writing but classes in dancing, music, and other arts.

The story hour is a favorite of children everywhere; here they listen to tales of Kantjil, the mouse-deer.

After a long night of entertainment in his honor, Harjanto is circumcised. The gamelan orchestra, below, is featured at major festivities.

This modern wajang show, part of a wedding entertainment, shows President Sukarno facing Musso, his Communist adversary in the Madiun revolt during the early days of the Republic.

Here is Seneng's father, who taught our daughter, Jill, the
intricacies of Java's Srimpi dance.

Buried beneath this modern printing press is a bull's head, to protect the newspaper from evil spirits. Below, students pore over magazines and books, cheap dregs of the American press, and attractive propaganda in English from Russia and China.

Gold and silver ornaments are a more traditional and trusted investment than village co-operatives and bank accounts. Below, people in need of cash bring their jewelry to the pawnshop, where the transaction is simple but interest rates high.

This farmer's tool-of-all-work, called a *patchul,* is worth about $1. If he has a plow, as below, his assets increase to $10. Two animals, worth perhaps $50 each, make him rich.

The author grips the handles of a plow just before the frenzied buffalo's dash across the rice paddies.

In Sumatra, there is no end of hard work clearing the jungle for more farm land and sawing wood. The pioneers feel the central government, in Java, is apathetic toward their problems.

FIVE

The Life and
Death of Sulisto

WHEN HE was five days old, Rahaju's son celebrated his first birthday. Eadie was included in my invitation and brought her copy of Dr. Spock's *Baby and Child Care* as a gift. Unable to read, Rahaju eagerly scanned the pictures. At first, shyness hushed the questions trembling on her lips. But soon the common joys and anxieties of motherhood dissolved the barriers between the two women. They sat in the sunshine crooning alternately over the infant and Dr. Spock, while, within the house, we males celebrated the fifth-day ceremony.

The *modin* asked why the celebration was being held.

"To give my son a name," said Djogo.

The religious man chanted, "A child has been born. The parents beg Allah to protect it from the *demits* and *danjangs,* the good and evil spirits that inhabit this house. The name they have chosen, may Allah be pleased, is Sulisto."

Samiek explained that Sulisto meant "clever" and addressed himself to the refreshments. Borrowed platters piled with rice covered the earthen floor. One large mound was for the dead.

Another was for Sulisto's afterbirth. A third was for the evil spirits, a fourth for the friendly ones. Another was for the neighborhood children lingering outside the door. Another, topped with eggs and pepper, was for the guests. A kerosene lamp, symbolizing the sun, omen of happiness, cast light on the lavish array.

A mingling of Islam and animism, it seemed, touched all Javanese ritual. No one minded that *demits* and *danjangs* contradicted Mohammed's insistence on one spirit, Allah. Animism, indeed, survived not only Islamic but also Western, scientific teaching. Months later I was to ask the director of Solo's biggest hospital whether he believed in spirits. This competent surgeon, trained in Holland's finest universities, said, very seriously, "Of course. I meet them often in my work. This very week I was called to a sick man's house. He lay dying, a wad of tobacco in his mouth. He would not remove the tobacco to answer my questions. His wife said it was because the moment he took out the wad, three *demits* tried to ram their fists down his throat. I instructed her to ask the *demits*, next time she saw them, why they attacked her husband. The following day she came to my office. The *demits* had said it was because the couple planned to move to another house, leaving them to starve. They promised to spare her husband if she placed seven piles of rice by the door. My prescription was to leave the rice for the *demits*. When I called again, the rice and wad of tobacco were gone, and the man was completely recovered."

At the moment, the economics of Sulisto's christening intrigued me as much as the animism. In addition to its eighty million human population, Indonesia, it appeared, was feeding countless gourmands from the spirit world. I wondered whether United Nations agricultural technicians laboring to improve the nation's nutrition reckoned on these invisible mouths and stomachs. I wondered, too, how Djogo's slender purse could afford such a feast and tried to compute the cost in dollars. At the official rate, a rupiah was worth nine cents; on the black market, three. Five cents struck me as a realistic average value. At that rate—one I was to use henceforth in all conversions of rupiahs into dollars—the delicacies on Djogo's floor cost about two dollars, almost half the sandal cobbler's monthly income. Djogo admitted borrowing the money from a usurer at four cents interest a day. "And," Samiek added, "this is just the beginning. Every thirty-five days of his first year, Sulisto will have another party."

On his thirty-fifth day, Sulisto's hair was cut. With his dried umbilical cord and first feces, the hair was weighed, the sum determining the weight of gold in his first ring. It was scarcely thicker than a thread and cost two dollars. Djogo's eyes shone as brightly as the gleaming metal. "It is gold," he whispered. "It is worth more than paper rupiahs."

Sulisto was unlike most American babies of his age. From the moment of birth, he looked old and wise. Rahaju carried him slung in a scarf so that his lips were never far from her nipple. He rarely soiled the scarf, wetting usually in a reclining position on a folded cloth Rahaju kept handy. He fattened on his diet of mother's milk and mashed banana, and in no time at all he was king of the kampong.

Over the weeks, while Sulisto nursed or slept at his mother's breast, Rahaju and Eadie talked nothing but babies. At Eadie's urging, Rahaju began at the beginning. She and Djogo had had intercourse for one purpose, conception. While farmers might occasionally copulate with their wives in the fields at planting time to encourage the seeds to multiply, and while certain men and women, Rahaju confessed, indulged for pleasure or money, married couples wanted babies. A woman who did not conceive visited a *dukun* for massage or a stiff dose of tapax liman, a common weed prescribed for most uterine disorders. Some of Rahaju's neighbors also practiced *sihir,* a science combining the powers of the heart, mind and spirit. By meditation before intercourse, followed by deep desire consciously applied during the sex act, they believed conception could be induced. In marriages truly built on love and ardor, *sihir* was instinctive and such unions were fruitful. When they weren't, husbands sometimes suspected coldness in their wives and, under Moslem law, could and did divorce them.

Bambang threw a reverse twist on the *sihir* theory. In his many affairs he rarely worried about conception because only pleasure or money was involved. The only precaution his lady friends took was to douche with *air belanda,* or Dutch water, as soda pop was locally called. When his own wife underwent an infertile phase, they consulted the sex manuals abounding in Solo's bookstalls. They also used the advertising mainstays of Indonesia's newspapers—Sexanol, Potensol, Pregnol and other patent medicines.

For ordinary kampong women, Rahaju made clear, aphrodisiacs and patent medicines were prohibitively expensive. They relied on the *dukun*'s extensive stock of *tjraken* or herbs. Not to conceive twice every three years during her childbearing period meant marital risk and public humiliation. Eadie and I began to understand what lay behind Indonesia's birth rate, the world's second highest, of close to a million full-term pregnancies a year.

Rahaju was shocked when Eadie mentioned contraception and abortion. Babies, she said, were wealth, like a buffalo or a horse. Each child brought its own quotient of good luck into the world and contributed it to that of the family as a whole. The more children, the more secure the parents in their old age.

The kampong, too, desired babies on the principle that "many children make the village strong." Above all, Rahaju affirmed, children were loved and wanted for themselves.

Samiek, who interpreted for Eadie during her visits with Rahaju, reduced the whole subject to a proverb: "Many children carry the parents high." By high, he meant both heaven and the upper social and economic strata. He said the Koran exhorted the faithful to be prolific and, thus, to propagate the faith. When Eadie herself became pregnant, he advised her to drop all talk of family planning. Rumors were going around, he warned, that she was seeking ways of doing away with her unborn baby.

After missing her first period, Rahaju had embarked on a careful regimen. Since a pregnant woman is unclean, since death in childbirth is commonplace, and since only clean persons can return to God, she had taken great pains with her toilet—bathing, washing her hair and cleaning her nails carefully. Every eight days she had eaten the seed of a long pepper, a gentle laxative. She had avoided the meat of animals born feet first, fish, which eats its own kind, game, which induces bleeding, and durian, a fruit known to cause abortion. Such abstention was to ease her confinement.

Her seventh month had been celebrated by a *tingkeban*. The bath stall had been decorated with flowers, and rice offerings had been placed on the ground for the spirits. After her bath, Djogo and his mother had smashed an egg and a coconut to encourage the rupture of the uterine membrane. Rahaju had rapidly donned and doffed seven sarongs, an additional inducement to a smooth delivery. The kampong had then consumed large quantities of ceremonial food. Altogether, the *tingkeban* had cost seven dollars.

For delivering Sulisto, the *dukun* charged fifty cents. A few kampong women had been to nursing homes, where the bill for delivery, dressings, and a week's care came to ten dollars. Compared with doctors, Rahaju said, even this was cheap. Doctors charged private patients as much as thirty dollars. Djogo added that the Communist Party leader in the kampong swore that this distinction between rich and poor was a disgrace to Indonesia. Djogo didn't seem disturbed that he had almost as much debt over his head as air. "What is more important," he asked, "debts or babies?"

Rahaju was as curious about Eadie's experiences as we were about hers. She could hardly believe Eadie's account of blood tests, vitamin diets, expensive layettes, hospital practices. When Eadie described how, after Jill and Arthur were born, a nurse had placed them in another room, she wept. "But why? How could she be so cruel?" Eadie explained about invisible germs from which infants must be protected. The light of understanding dawned in Rahaju's eyes. "Of course," she exclaimed. *"Demits!"*

She too had taken precautions against "invisible germs." An oil lamp had been placed beside the baby, its light dissuading the *demits* from coming near. When the umbilical stump was dry and ready to fall off, relatives had carried Sulisto in their arms, never leaving him untended for a moment. A stone pestle used for grinding corn had been painted and dressed to resemble a baby and placed in his usual spot on the floor, to deceive the spirits, invite their attack and spare Sulisto.

Rahaju was delighted to learn that Eadie, during her pregnancies, had been prey to vagrant appetites. She told how she had sent Djogo out at midnight to pick the coconuts she craved from the tallest trees. She rejoiced when Eadie described how American hospitals were copying the Javanese idea of allowing babies to room in with their mothers, instead of sealing them off behind glass. She was flattered when Eadie insisted on learning the lullaby she sang to Sulisto. The song was as old as Java.

> *I am caressing you,*
> *Child of the lilac deer.*
> *I am caressing you,*
> *Child of the day,*
> *Sleeping like a stone,*
> *Like a stone of a mountain,*
> *Like a stick of sempu wood.*

The lullaby was reputed to have hypnotic effect on babies. When Eadie tried it on Arthur, though without success, the whole kampong buzzed with the compliment.

Djogo practiced another form of hypnosis on Sulisto called *kudangan.* Evenings, after work, he would dandle the boy on his knee and talk earnestly to him about his future. "You are a clever baby. You will fly the fastest pigeons. You will own many hectares of land." Occasionally a neighbor squatted beside Djogo. "*Pak,*" he would say, "you should change your baby talk. Tell your son not to be servile. Tell him we fought to throw out the *belandas.* Tell him when he grows up he must fight to rid our country of the outsiders who still own our oil and rubber." He kept urging Djogo to join the one group that cared about Sulisto's future, the Communist Party. "Communism," he said, "is better than *kudangan.*"

Sulisto's future was Rahaju's uppermost thought. With independence, she felt, all things were possible. He could go to school and choose a better vocation than his father's. The choice would be made when he was eight months old. The grandmother would guide Sulisto's first step, placing his foot on a ladder made of bananas and sugar cane, to insure a sweet

59

life. Next, the baby would be placed in a cock's cage, with a pot filled with rice and many objects. Whatever Sulisto took from the pot would portend his future. Rice meant he would be an official. A gold coin meant he might be a moneylender; a pencil meant a career as a teacher. Then, dressed in new clothing, Sulisto would receive his first real toys.

Rahaju took the toys from their hiding place. One was a puppet of Arjuna, favorite of the wajang's five princes. The other was a rocket-firing jeep.

Sulisto died on his ninetieth day. Rahaju's milk had dried early, and she had begun to feed him a gruel of rice and water from the stream that coursed the kampong. Sulisto's stool turned loose and green. The *dukun* mixed an infusion of the bitter, aromatic tubers of *teki,* a weed growing wild around the area. There was some improvement, but Djogo decided to take the baby to the Polyclinic in Djebres, a not-too-distant town. The queue before the outpatient department was long, the sun hot, the street dusty. When Sulisto's turn came, there was no doctor to treat him. Instead, a clerk gave Djogo pills for Sulisto to take every three hours with water.

When they returned, Sulisto was sicker than ever. The *dukun,* enraged by Djogo's faithlessness, would have nothing further to do with the matter. In three days, Sulisto was dead.

The signal drum outside the house of the kampong's headman was pounded. Friends left for the cemetery to dig a small grave. Sulisto's hands were crossed over his breast and his face was turned toward Mecca. The *modin* whispered in his right ear, "There is but one God and Mohammed is His Prophet."

Relatives walked ahead of the coffin, scattering coins at every crossroad until the cortege reached the cemetery. An uncle shielded the little box from the sun with a parasol. The body was removed from the coffin and placed on a shelf dug into the side of the grave. Mourners tossed in handfuls of earth and intoned:

> *I made you from earth.*
> *I return you to earth.*
> *I shall take you from the earth*
> *Once more again.*

Rahaju did not weep. She returned to the house and sat in a corner, hunched as though she were cold. Neighbors dropped in to offer their condolences. Among the first was the money-lender. He urged Djogo not to worry about the money he owed. "Just try," he said, "to keep up the interest payments."

The leader of the local Moslem Party tried to comfort the father. "It is Allah's will. You are young. You will have many children." The Moslem Women's Organization brought a gift of rice. The chairlady of Perwari, the Indonesian Women's Association, brought a length of white cotton cloth. The president of the kampong's collective pressed a few rupiahs into Djogo's hand. The next-door neighbor waited until the others left. Then he sat with Rahaju and Djogo in the dark house and talked. Weeks later, Djogo told me what he said.

"Sulisto did not need to die. In another kind of society, he would have lived. There would have been doctors, medicines, everything now reserved for the rich. Djogo, wake up! For Sulisto's sake, join the struggle for a Communist Indonesia. Fight beside us so that your next son may live."

SIX

Harjanto's Circumcision

OUR HOUSEBOY'S NAME was Sindo. Short, swarthy, middle-aged, he was the most self-effacing man we had ever known. Each morning he appeared from nowhere, dressed in white singlet, gray shorts and a black velvet Moslem cap which, in all the time he worked for us, he never took off. Each evening, after dinner, he vanished into the smoky kampong behind our house. During the day, whenever his duties brought him near us, he cringed into a half-bow and shuffled out of our way on soundless bare feet. Watching him, Eadie and I used to speculate, irrationally, on whether he was bald, or whether the hair hidden beneath the oversize cap was black or grizzled. We never found out. We also wondered what kind of man Sindo really was, and what kind of life he led when he left us. As weeks went by, without a clue, Sindo became a challenge. If we couldn't crack the façade of our own houseboy, our mission was a failure.

In the matter of cracking façades, all the advantages lay with Sindo. We were denied access to his life, while he missed little of what went on in ours. He betrayed no reaction to our manner of living, except that he clearly approved the love and care we lavished on Jill and Arthur. Soon, indeed, between him and them, a warm friendship developed. They chattered constantly in some lingua franca of their own, incomprehensible to grown-ups.

Eadie and I were close to the point of despair when, one morning, we received a letter from, of all people, Sindo. At the moment he was in the bathroom, killing cockroaches with a scantling broom. His energetic swishing and thwacking relieved our momentary anxiety that the letter bore ill tidings. It turned out to be an invitation, handsomely lettered in script, that retained in Samiek's translation much of the majesty of the original high Javanese. It read:

DEAR SIR,

With this I inform you, may Allah bless us, that next Saturday I intend to circumcise my son, Harjanto. The circumcision will take place at seven o'clock in the morning with all simplicity. If you are so minded, and have no other engagements, I invite you and your lady to honor my house in Kampong Baru with your visit on the previous night, Friday, Heaven Nymphs Night, for the purpose of blessing and giving pleasure to my son, and to partake of whatever refreshments may be offered. And at the same time you are invited to enjoy some wajang fragments, and to listen to gamelan music. Full of hope, I expect your arrival. Yours faithfully,

SINDOESOWARNO AND WIFE.

I went to the bathroom door. "Congratulations, Sindo, on the birth of your son."

Sindo took several seconds to consider this remark. "Tuan," he said, "my son was born twelve years ago."

"But Sindo, we have just received your invitation to his circumcision. In my country, boys are circumcised a few days after birth."

"So soon?" Sindo asked. "What can be the meaning of circumcision in your country?"

"It is a matter of health. And a newborn infant feels no pain."

"To us," said Sindo, "circumcision has another meaning. Moslems remember that God told Abraham to shed the blood of his son, Ishmael. Abraham made ready to sacrifice his son at God's command. Unless a boy is old enough to understand this and to consent to shed his blood for God, his circumcision can have no meaning. At twelve, Harjanto will suffer pain and thereby show his love of Allah."

On Heaven Nymphs Night, following Sindo's directions, I turned off at the prison and entered one of the grassy lanes leading to Kampong Baru. It lay on the city's fringe, throbbing with gamelan music and glowing in the light of coconut-oil lanterns. The porch of the kampong's biggest house had been converted into a stage, covered with rugs and brilliantly lighted. About two hundred guests crowded about, the men comfortably seated on benches ranged in front, the women and children standing on either side. I hardly recognized Sindo in his formal attire—wing collar, tie, and black cutaway worn above a sarong. Smiling and erect, he greeted me without a trace of subservience and led me to a choice seat, flanked by men whom he introduced as his brother and the chairman of the kampong's Culture Club. Behind me I heard whispered inquiries about who I was, and the answer. *"Belanda*—Dutchman! *American* Dutchman!"

A red moon, barely risen above the treetops, signaled the start of the festivities. The president of the *rukun desa,* social-welfare organization of the ward, greeted the assemblage. He reminded it that, when Sindo had been unemployed, he had sworn an oath that as soon as he found work he would give a *salamatan*, a party, for the kampong. Tonight the promise was about to be redeemed. In witness thereof, he dropped a coconut leaf filled with yellow rice. As the package broke open on the floor, the audience murmured approval.

Next, a friend expressed, on Sindo's behalf, gratitude to all who had troubled to attend this modest celebration. He begged forgiveness for anything that might displease the guests, and for the poor quality of the refreshment. The chairman of the Culture Club leaned toward me and whispered. "It is customary for the host to let others speak for him. Only fools praise themselves or push themselves forward."

A girl appeared on the stage, her face masked with the sweet resignation of the blind. A violinist and flutist provided a slow, haunting accompaniment as she sang the plaintive *krontjong* and *langgam* love songs of the people.

> *Though far from my eyes,*
> *You remain in my mind.*
> *It is long since we parted.*
> *My tears are falling.*
> *Oh, if only you would send me*
> *Word of your love.*
> *Give it to the wind that is blowing.*
> *Send me your heart on a passing cloud.*

The Culture Club chairman sighed. *"Krontjong* is dying. Our boys and girls are turning to your own country's music. Boogie-woogie, they call it." He smiled ruefully as he pronounced the strange words. "But *krontjong*, after all, is not really ours. Portuguese sailors brought it here four hundred years ago. Our own music is *Gending Gede*, the classical music of Java. Every kampong has a gamelan orchestra which plays it. Kampong

Baru's has twenty-seven pieces. Tonight you will learn why it is known as the best in the province."

As the gamelan murmured its first phrases, Sindo reappeared with a wisp of a man he introduced as Slamet, a master of gamelan, a teacher of *Gede*. Slamet took over the seat and duties of the culture chairman. "Sindo tells me you are an American," he said. "Do you have good music in America—music like the *Gede*, which expresses the history and philosophy of our people? No one knows how *Gede* began, except that the first Javanese suffused it with their animist worship of the tree. Root, trunk, branch and flower—one beginning, one growth, one design, together, expressive of life. Hinduism added melody. Buddhism quickened the tempo. Islam slowed it, giving it dignity and depth."

Slamet's low voice caught the music's rhythm and excitement. "Listen! The gong and the flute are saying to the others: 'We choose this key!' The violin replies: 'I choose this melody.' The drum acknowledges their selection and strikes the beat. Now the drum is the conductor. With the xylophones, it plays the stress tones, the fixed rhythm underlying both music and life. The other instruments improvise within the stress tones. Like society, the orchestra is a collective thing. But within it, each musician must go his way alone, living his own life, seeking by himself his own expressions of beauty, but never departing from the master design."

The music, mounting toward a climax, was matched by the intensity of Slamet's words. "In this combination of the fixed and the free, our people sense life's meaning. Within a fixed, repeated rhythm—birth and death, youth and age, sunrise and sunset—there come and go the individual personality's development, sadness and joy, poverty and prosperity, the wave's ever-changing, ever repeating form. Each drop of water, each drop

66

of blood, moves in its own rhythm, within a greater rhythm. And in the end, the sea calms, the heart stops, the music ends."

A single voice, ranging from a woman's falsetto to a rumbling bass, rose above the fading music.

When you are a leader of the people
You must be humble.
You must know men's character.
If you choose a teacher,
Seek one who is honest,
One who suffers, who does not expect
rewards for what he does.

The last echo melted into the night. When Slamet spoke again, his voice was apologetic. "Forgive me if I have talked too much. But unless you understand *Gede,* you cannot understand our people. Nor can you understand how some of us feel as we watch our youth beguiled and corrupted by America's music. We cannot print *Gede* in cheap booklets. We cannot sell it for so many rupiahs a tune, as you are doing in every bookstall in our province. There is no score. There are no lyrics. There is no picture of a naked actress. There is nothing except what is in the hearts and souls of an aggrieved people. What you have heard can never be heard again. No two lives are the same. Nor two melodies."

The moon was high. Somewhere, in one of the houses, Harjanto was sitting in chilled water, numbing his penis to ease the pain of his impending circumcision. But here, among the guests, the refreshment and entertainment went on without stint. A troupe of boys not yet in their teens began a slow, studied movement of heads, eyes and hands. I asked Slamet whether the dance of Java held as much hidden significance as its music. Once again, a rebuke edged his reply.

"With us, dancing is not a matter of moving the body in response to music, for sensual enjoyment. Animals do that. We are human beings, with hearts, minds, souls and dignity. Our dance expresses calmness, control, concern with life and God. Watch the dancers. They rise and look straight ahead, arms outstretched. Whatever a man does in life, he must first know the purpose and direction of his action. They walk now in circles, to examine the world's offerings. Looking right and left, they recognize good and evil. In flipping their scarves, they cast off life's difficulties by their own strength and will. Their eyes move from side to side, the head motionless—to center all faculties in the mind and link them with the heart. They touch hand to sword. The scabbard is the body, the kris is the soul. When you know this, you know yourself, you know all."

My other neighbor added: "The music represents the world. A man must keep in step with the world. In a revolutionary world, a man must be a revolutionary. Our children learn never to go against the music, never to go against the rhythm of the world."

Fingering the food from the banana leaf set before me, I mulled over the evening's meaning. Almost everything these people did was suffused with political awareness. The dignity of man, the unity of life, were here reaffirmed in dance and music. While not all could express themselves with Slamet's skill, an infinitely rich philosophy was widely shared. Also it was threatened. I sensed again the oneness of these people with their culture, and the recklessness of any action that did not respect it.

Men now walked about, snuffing all lamps but one which threw its light on a large white screen. An old man, the *dalang,* knelt before it, arranging the puppets which comprised the cast of the wajang fragment promised in Sindo's invitation. To his left ranged the villains, large and pink-complexioned. To his right were the heroes, small and black—a neat reversal of what some Westerners would deem appropriate. As the puppets were lifted into the lamplight, their shadows raced across the screen. The *dalang* sang:

> *It is not easy for a man to live*
> *Who does not know how to live.*
> *Such a man is like a carabao.*
> *But a carabao is worth more than he.*
> *One can eat the flesh of a carabao.*
> *One cannot eat the flesh of a man.*

Tonight's story was about a wedding feast, celebrated in a mythical kingdom by five ruling princes. The feast has lasted night and day, for month after month. In their craving for rice, women and wine, the noblemen have forgotten their duties to the people, who groan under the heavy weight of taxation levied to pay for the orgy. Their servant, Semar—the fat, foolish clown after whom Arthur had been nicknamed—reproaches the princes and is thrashed for his impudence. When a blow lands on his head, Semar, suddenly furious, cries out: "You go your way. We will go ours!"

Semar and two fellow clowns and servants, transformed into warriors, attack and defeat the princes. Only the minister, Kresno, escapes. After long meditation in a forest, Kresno perceives the princes' sin. Returning to the palace, he kneels before the three warriors and promises that if the princes are released they will govern righteously. Kresno's humility has magic effect. The warriors revert to servants and the princes return to the palace, to rule thereafter with justice and wisdom. I recognized the source of Seneng's little speech to Arthur. Slamet paid me the compliment of refraining from explanation.

The shadows on the screen paled as dawn crept into the kampong. Yet one more brief story was presented, a popular play based on Javanese legend. It dealt with a prince, Djoko Tingkir, journeying with his bodyguards to a neighboring kingdom. In the deepest part of a river he was beset by alligators. Their king, a huge white beast, lunged at Djoko's raft. Djoko seemed doomed, but in a paroxysm of strength and fury he lifted the alligator over his head, pulled out his tongue, and tossed him, dead, into the river. The other alligators fled, and Djoko continued his journey.

The time had finally come for Harjanto's ordeal. A slender lad, handsome in a new coat and sarong, he followed his father to an ivory-bamboo chair, flanked by flowers and rice offerings to the spirit. The *bong*, a religious man specializing in circumcisions, asked the boy to repeat the familiar prayer: "There is but one God and Mohammed is His Prophet." Sindo's brother sat in the chair, took Harjanto in his lap, and covered the lad's eyes with his hands. The *bong* held the foreskin between bamboo sticks, cut it deftly, and bandaged the wound with lint. Guests crowded around to congratulate Harjanto on his new status as a Moslem and a man. Harjanto blinked away his tears and smiled.

Sindo and I walked home together. With his singlet and shorts, he had donned again his servile manner. After apologizing for the poverty of his entertainment, he voiced the hope that his friends had added to my understanding and enjoyment. "Not always has Indonesia been free," he added. "For many years it was dangerous for us to speak in ways our masters could understand. We therefore discovered ways of unburdening our hearts in music, dances and plays that no *belanda* could comprehend. It is a habit hard to break."

I admitted that without the help of his friends most of the inner meaning of what I had seen would have escaped me. "Not all your entertainment is as simple," I said, "as the story of Djoko Tingkir."

Days later I passed a store displaying crude paintings of popular wajang and *ketoprak* legends. Among them was one of Djoko struggling with the white alligator. It made a nice souvenir, one I could explain to friends without becoming too involved in cryptic symbolism. I bought it and hung it on our living-room wall, where it was much admired by the children. When Sindo shuffled in with his broom, they insisted that he tell them the story.

"It is about a prince," he said, "who met a village girl in his travels. He made love to her and left her with a baby. The village people were angry because the powerful prince had betrayed an innocent maiden. But since he was a nobleman, and they just poor farmers, how could they punish him? They consulted a *dukun,* who transformed them into alligators. When the prince came down the river on his raft, they attacked him and would have killed him if he had not succeeded in pulling out the tongue of their chief, the big white alligator. To pull out a tongue means to give a bribe—and that is what had happened. The prince had bribed the village headman, and the maiden was never avenged."

SEVEN

"Let Us Do It Together"

N EVER AGAIN, after Sulisto's death, could Eadie and I see
Asia's infant-death rate as a cold statistic. We knew now
its meaning in terms of human joy and sorrow. We had
learned that even a dead baby fueled communism's thrust toward power. We had glimpsed the hopelessness of Djogo's
economic outlook. The weight of despair that burdened Rahaju's heart lay heavily upon us. We wondered how the texture
of Asian life, at Djogo's level, could be repaired and strength-
ened so as to prevent such human waste and forestall such
resentments.

It was while our desire to help and to heal burned most
intensely that I read in a Djakarta newspaper about the United
States Congress debating a two-hundred-million-dollar aid program for undeveloped Asian countries. In a land where two
hundred dollars represented a fair annual income for a family
of eight, two hundred million dollars is impressive. And Indonesia lay directly in the path of this mighty green flood. It had
a better than even chance to divert several millions into its
parched economy. Here was a rare chance to see for myself what
happened among the kampong people when Uncle Sam brand-
ished his bankroll in their direction.

As the only Americans in the area, Eadie and I braced our-selves for the jubilation the news would surely evoke among our neighbors. But days passed, the paragraph so carefully clipped from the newspaper became rumpled, and local interest in America continued to focus on our mistreatment of Negroes and Indians, our lust for kissing and killing, and the private life of Marilyn Monroe. I was finally forced to broach the sub-ject to a neighbor, owner of a small wood-milling plant. He read the clipping and shook his head. "Most of us," he ex-plained, "are private businessmen and farmers. This is a matter between governments. What has it to do with me?"

Several of his workmen, superb but illiterate craftsmen, also seemed puzzled. "Newspapers," said their spokesmen, "are for the big cities, the educated, the rich. We workers learn about the world's affairs in the market place, or in the social room of our union. If this news concerned us, it would by now be on everybody's tongue. But tongues are silent on matters they can-not grasp. What are two hundred million dollars? What is *one* dollar in rice? And is Indonesia an undeveloped country? That cannot be, for this very town is the hub of the universe. No culture is more developed than ours."

A farmer rested his buffalo as he pondered the matter. "But American aid," he finally said, "is no longer news. We have known about it for years. It is a favorite joke in our kampong. Even my son, who is not yet twelve, has heard about the ma-chines from America to be given to us as proof of your pity. We all know that somehow the gift from America costs a farmer more than he would pay in a store. Even the dullest man among us knows where your dollars go—to the Chinese, the grafters, the rich. Forgive me, but our hearts do not beat joy-fully at the promise of America's money."

Among educated Indonesians, reactions ranged from polite

73

pleasure to doubt, gloom and fear. A teacher in a nearby voca-
tional school agreed that American dollars could help build the
dams, roads, and powerhouses the country needed. "But," she
added, "even we who most yearn to modernize Indonesia flinch
at accepting America's dollars. Why? As children we learned to
distrust a stranger who gives something to another, for he gives
to place the other under obligation. As colonials, we saw the
Dutch build schools, hospitals and orphanages, piously claiming
they were for the people. But for everything they gave, we paid
a bitter price in rice and liberty. We called such acts 'ethical
policy.' American aid reminds us of 'ethical policy'—sinister
purposes cloaked with charity."

The district tax collector looked out of his window at the
busy street, filled with barefoot pedicab drivers, shabby visitors
from the countryside, mothers on their way to market. "In a
poor place like this," he said, "dollars are dangerous. Only the
Chinese among us understand their nature and power, how to
manipulate them and, in the end, to monopolize them. Most of
us understand commodities, not cash. Five years after your dollars arrive, will they be in the hands of the farmers, the Co-
operatives, the village organizations through which our people
are striving to raise and manage capital? Or in the coffers of a
shrewd, worldly few?"

Concern darkened the eyes behind the spectacles as he continued. "You Americans have a saying, 'Money is the root of
evil.' If that is true in a society like yours, with its vast machinery to manage money, in a climate like ours it can strangle
every ideal we fought for in our revolution. Only if dollars can
be grafted to the root, trunk and branch of Indonesian life can
they bear nourishing fruit, instead of poison."

To examine the root, trunk and branch of Indonesian life,
Samiek, Bambang and I chose Bekonan, a village of a thousand-

odd families, mostly farmers, artisans, merchants and small industrialists, principally manufacturers of cheap batik. It was not
as well off as some villages where the soil was richer, nor as
poor, perhaps, as the poverty-ridden communities of western
Java. Like most of Indonesia's land, Bekonan's was locally
owned, with little landlessness and tenancy. Most holdings averaged less than a quarter-acre. From them the owners forced
two rice crops a year, plus one cash crop such as tobacco, plus
one catch crop such as corn. From the soil, plus what they
earned in cottage industry, or shopkeeping, or repairing bicycles, families eked an annual income of $160. Eight persons
comprised an average family.

Bekonan had no electricity, machinery, modern methods.
But, because the village was blessed with a benign climate and
nature's prodigality, few families knew hunger. The village was
almost self-sufficient, lacking only salt and cloth. A bamboo-
shaded island in a sea of paddy fields, it carried on much as it
had for ages, old-fashioned and poor, yet, it turned out, resilient
and astir with freedom's fresh impulses.

The *lurah* or headman served us tea on the porch of his
house. After reading the letter of introduction from the Regent
of the province with which Samiek had had the foresight to arm
us, he made a brief speech summing up Bekonan's exact position. "Individually," he said, "our people are too poor to cope
with droughts and locusts, earthquakes and floods. Since earliest
times, we have worked out ways of overcoming these dangers
as a group. While the Dutch were here, we conformed to their
system on the surface. But beneath, we clung to our own ways
of life. Through these ancient institutions, we managed to
maintain our self-respect as human beings. And so they became
more precious to us than ever. Since independence, we seek not

75

to abolish or replace them, but to modernize and strengthen them. For they are the secret of our survival."

The secret of Bekonan's thousand-year survival as a community turned out to be the *rukun desa,* the village collective. Samiek translated its slogan, *Gotong rojong,* as "Let us do it together." Almost as old as Java, the collective endured through five major military and cultural invasions, from the Hindu to the Japanese. Tough and adaptable, it had always fulfilled the people's need for self-government and self-expression. It remained today the basic civic unit to which every family, rich or poor, belonged.

When a house burned and a family needed shelter, food and clothing, the collective supplied them. When a farmer fell ill, the collective harvested his crop for him. When a member was broke, the collective offered credit up to ten dollars, or it solicited from its membership the equivalent in seed, tools and animal power. Each household had one vote at the monthly meetings, electing officers, budgeting income and expenses, managing village affairs in democratic, voluntary association with its neighbors.

Five years ago, the popularly elected *lurah* had summoned the villagers to discuss a new idea. Holding up a twig, he said: "One twig can easily be broken. Many twigs together are strong. This we have learned from the *rukun desa.* Now it is time to apply the lesson to our business affairs. Each of us keeps what he has and manages his own land or shop. But each puts a little into a common fund. We use the fund to buy seed cheaply at harvest time. We store our rice, selling it at a higher price in planting time. We put the profits back into the fund. Little by little, through saving and wise investment, we raise our own capital. Then we make this capital work for us, like a buffalo or a mule."

The villagers, after long discussion, agreed to give the idea a trial. Naming the new co-operative the United Action of the People of Bekonan, 192 farmers paid dues, equivalent to 75 cents, entitling each to a maximum of one voting share. Since most homes lacked cash, housewives skimmed one spoonful of rice from each day's food allotment and placed it in a separate bag. When the bags were full, husbands brought them to the co-operative's granary. A fund of rice worth 150 dollars was formed and was matched by a government loan at 8-per-cent annual interest.

For the first time in any man's memory, Bekonan had capital. It amounted to only 300 dollars, but it was a beginning. Members borrowed seed at planting time, when it was scarce, repaying it at harvest time when rice was abundant. One hundred rupiahs' worth of rice in the dry season was valued at 150 in the wet. In a position to wait for high prices, the United Action held on until, by majority vote, the paddy was wholesaled in a nearby city at a 50-per-cent profit.

Recently the United Action divided among its members half of its profits. Part of the remainder was added to capital reserve, part was invested. Other village co-operatives bought motor trucks to carry crops to distant markets where prices are higher, or they stocked improved seed and tools. Bekonan's voted to build a road between the village and the highway, so that, with future profits, it too might buy a Chevrolet and market its rice wherever it commanded the highest prices.

The chairman of the co-operative explained that occasionally, in some villages, judgment had been bad, or a sorely tempted official had absconded, or earthquake and flood had doomed the best human effort. But generally, as in Bekonan, he said, the people's experiment in self-generation of capital promised success. The number of Indonesia's co-operatives had risen to over ten thousand, with close to two million members and a total capital of five million dollars. Vice-President Mohammed Hatta was dedicated to their continued growth. Last year, at the opening of the Republic's first school to train farmers in co-operative management, he pronounced them "the beginnings of industrial Indonesia."

Already, in Bekonan, industrialization had begun. The faint smell of burning charcoal, of molten wax, of boiling dyestuffs, proclaimed the existence of a cottage industry producing the people's favorite fabric, batik. Cottage workers picked up the bleached cambric from a privately owned factory, applied the wax design, and delivered the cloth for final processing at the plant. The factory owner had joined the Indonesian Batik Co-operative Association, one of the largest of the Republic's industrial co-operatives. Membership was voluntary, costing the owner fifty dollars. In addition, he paid ten cents on every five dollars' worth of cambric and dyestuff he bought through the Association. Distribution of the finished batik remained the owner's responsibility, but sizable savings resulted from co-operative purchasing. A union of cottage workers, an adjunct of the Masjumi or Moslem Party, had negotiated an agreement with the factory owner; workers now shared in these savings.

Other villages had set up charcoal factories, or pottery plants, or other small privately owned industries, which, in turn, were branching out into small *induks,* or industrial co-operatives. The trend to a growth economy, in both farming and manufacturing, seemed strong and infectious. It extended, among others, to Bekonan's merchants, carpenters, bicycle repairmen and other small artisans and entrepreneurs.

Once a week, on the porch of the town hall, a storekeeper set up the office of the village bank, created, funded and managed by Bekonan's businessmen. To be eligible for credit, and to share in profits, a borrower must own his own business and must buy shares—ten was maximum for any one member—at fifty cents per voting share. Members paid 10-per-cent interest on short-term loans, 40-per-cent on loans of a year. Profits were reckoned annually, with one quarter paid into the village treasury, a quarter added to the bank's reserves, and half divided among shareholders.

In local voluntary purchasing, marketing, and banking co-operatives like Bekonan's, I learned, thousands of men and women who never before had saved, invested and profited from the judicious management of capital were learning the meaning of a growth economy, in which a little sacrifice today reaped dividends tomorrow. They were exhilarated more by the sense of dignity and hope imparted by the experience than by any actual prosperity which, at this early stage, was limited. For self-generation of capital, adequate to Indonesia's needs, was slow.

Meanwhile, other indigenous economic practices, deep-rooted and malignant, sapped the people's strength. Bekonan, like every other village, ruefully repeated an old adage: "The sun is hot but 2 per cent is hotter." The 2 per cent referred to interest charged by the village moneylenders, reckoned daily. Nothing was easier than borrowing money from a usurer to celebrate a birth, a circumcision, a wedding or a death. No collateral was demanded. No papers had to be signed. No fine print had to be read. But for every five dollars he borrowed for a year, a man obligated himself to pay back $36.50.

Bekonan also had a *rumah gadai*, or pawnshop. Two, in fact —one official, one private. So had every village of any size in the Republic. Everyone who had a sarong, a bicycle, or a brace-let, and who needed money, eventually joined the queues be-fore their windows. Trained appraisers quickly paid out less

79

than half the article's value in cash, plus a receipt. Seven months to one year were allowed for redemption, with officially sanctioned interest ranging from 18 per cent for the shorter to 36 per cent for the longer period. In private pawnshops, these rates doubled. Compared with the usurer's, the *rumah gadai*'s rates were not high. Compared with dealing with a commercial bank, procedures were simple. Above all, villagers liked the *rumah gadai* because transactions related to tangible items and were therefore comprehensible. For tangible commodities, not cash, were what people understood and trusted.

Everyone in Bekonan remembered 1946, when one hundred rupiahs suddenly were worth one; 1949, when fifty new rupiahs were exchangeable for one newer rupiah; 1951, when the value of money was halved again. Ever since, money had bought less and less. Every villager deduced a simple truth: Only fools trust money. Wise men spend money as fast as they earn it, on cloth, jewelry, or anything one can feel, use and pawn.

Today, Bekonan's people were struggling to regain their confidence in cash. They were also striving for confidence in themselves. Confidence grew with each successful transaction, with each accretion and division of profit, with each visible proof that they could survive and prosper in the unfamiliar world of modern finance. It ebbed whenever bigger, smarter commercial banks, or richer, less scrupulous, big-city operators beat them at the strange and risky game. Each report of corruption in government, each rumor about overnight millionaires in the import-license racket, each upward swirl in the inflationary cycle lessened their belief in money, and in their own ability to survive in a capitalist world.

Word from abroad of multi-million dollar bonanzas, when and if it reached them, aroused new doubts and questions. "How will this foreign money affect our co-operative?" "Will any of it come down to us?' "Will it stay in the cities, in the big banks, among the politicians?" "Will the rich get richer?" "In this upper-class society of dollars and bankers and officials, do *we* belong?"

I searched for signs that America heard these questions. Finding none in Bekonan, I ranged the province, seeking evidence that American aid was down at the rice roots with the people, fused with them, one with them, laboring with them to build their own economic institutions, to generate their own capital growth—to make increased production not an end in itself, but a means to the Indonesia the people themselves desired. Nowhere was my search successful.

Most often, knowledge of American aid was absent. Where it was known, I heard Communists ask whether the increased production which America urged was for Indonesia or America. They reminded the people of 'ethical policy.' Subtly, they inched toward positions of influence in the collective and the co-operative, which, with sure instinct, they recognized as the hard-rock foundations of Indonesia's power. *"Gotong rojong,"* I heard one cry. "Let us do it together! That is the slogan of our collective. That is the essence of communism. What better proof that communism was born in Indonesia, belongs in Indonesia and must rule Indonesia!"

Marshaled against him were the deep-rooted wisdom of the people, their religious conviction, their ugly experience with Communist brutality in the ill-starred Madiun revolt against the Republic in 1948, and the anti-Communist sentiment of other political parties. "Think!" the president of Bekonan's collective urged the members one evening. "Everything we do together we do freely, by majority vote. Under communism, we would be forced to do it, by order of a small minority. *Gotong rojong* is pure democracy. Let us keep it that way."

The United States had no voice at these village councils. Neither did I, except to answer an occasional question which revealed, in stark clarity, the people's ignorance of twentieth-century capitalism. But it seemed to me that America's role was crucial. In design, content, distribution, did dollar aid give weight to Communist lies? Or, by clearly refuting them, did it strengthen the hand of democracy's defenders? Could it be conceived, at its source, to nourish the budding growth economy of the village? Or must it, by its seemingly exclusive emphasis on production, its aloofness from indigenous economic organisms, raise doubt as to whom production will benefit? Could American aid be expressed in terms of local values and understanding? Or must it, by some baleful necessity, be mouthed in the jargon of bankers and brokers? The absence of encouragement on these matters, coupled with my ignorance of economic affairs, suggested a visit to Djakarta, headquarters of American aid in Indonesia. There I found many realistic men and women as deeply disturbed as I.

A Foreign Operations official explained how American aid was then administered. "Their Cabinet sits around a table. Each minister submits a list of what he wants. The Minister of Plans consolidates them and draws up a program based on how much he thinks we're prepared to give. Then we go over it. We realize that to turn down any minister's request is to make an enemy of that minister. Since we're here to make friends, we generally go along with what they ask. We wind up with a patchwork program that panders to ministerial politics and pride.

"Does it necessarily bolster economic institutions at the rice roots? Does it ease credit? Does it undermine usury and the pawnshop habit? I doubt it. We don't know much, really, about the people. We're too tied up in administrative duties to get out

82

to the villages and learn. Without such knowledge, we're never in a position to discuss village problems with the ministers, or to suggest a program which we firmly believe to be responsive to village needs. Yet I am convinced that if we did, the ministers would be patriotic enough to buy it."

An agricultural economist, veteran of many foreign-aid campaigns in Asia, mopped his forehead, reddened either by Djakarta's humidity or by the heat engendered by the topic. "The Asian farmer and worker is now a voter. What he thinks is the key to Asia's future. A lot of us in this foreign-operations business know it. But Congress, not we, passes foreign-aid legislation. Never, in all the years I've been connected with aid programs, have we had a clean-cut Congressional mandate to find out what the farmer wants, and get it to him.

"When our orders arrive, they deal with dollars, tonnages, production statistics. And that's how we're supposed to render our accounts. It is easier to gauge the success of an operation in terms of tons of fertilizer than in terms of human attitudes. Too bad, because I've seen what happens to too much of that fertilizer. It is handed out, not in relation to soil needs, but so many tons per province, whether needed or not. Farmers throw it on the ground and burn their crops. That finishes the fertilizer. It also finishes American aid. Expensive breeding stock is also wasted. Machinery rusts in the fields. Sixty million rupiahs' worth of tractors is rotting right now in Borneo. We're so tied up in salvaging that mess, in bookkeeping and politics, we've lost the whole point and purpose of foreign aid—to help the people, the village people, to strengthen their own economic institutions along democratic lines."

A United States Information Agency specialist added: "When press releases on Asian aid arrive from Washington, we're equipped to pass them on to the local newspapers. Inter-

83

pret them in popular terms? Relate our aid to village values? Use indigenous channels of communication? Quit kidding! Instead of reaching the people on their own wave length, we're simply talking to a few intellectuals, politicians and ourselves."

Almost everyone agreed that American aid to Indonesia—and to Asia—was on the target. It was scoring scattered hits in the outer political and intellectual circles. But the big black bull's-eye in dead center—the people—was missed completely. Why didn't Washington take better aim? A top-level attaché smiled grimly.

"That is the only real mystery left in the not-so-mysterious East. It's hard to say. Time after time Washington calls us home for conferences. We fly back on fire with all we've seen and heard. We sit down in a steam-heated conference room, wearing coats and ties. Outside we see the city, the traffic, the office buildings, the well-stocked shops. Suddenly the villages, the people of Asia fade away.

"In that atomic environment, you feel foolish talking in terms of buffalo muscle and water wheels. All the same, you wait for your chance. It comes, everyone listens and then there's a silence. Finally someone says, 'Okay, let's get back to business.' Soon you're sunk in appropriation problems, administrative procedures, departmental reports. You find yourself competing with others in your glowing account of tonnages delivered and dollars spent. On the way back to your post, you kick yourself and wonder what happened. Is it just that it's more realistic to base programs on statistics than it is to base them on social and cultural factors? Or is it that, deep down, some of us have nothing in our hearts but contempt for brown-skinned farmers up to their knees in mud, and fear of such Communist-sounding things as people's collectives and co-operatives?"

84

Before leaving Djakarta, I asked some friends in the Embassy and in the business community to set down the ingredients of a sound economic policy for Asia. Their formula boiled down to this:

"Know the people, their pride in their country, their culture, and their own economic and other institutions. Know that they are private enterprisers and individualists, eager to raise their own capital and generate their own growth economy through their own collective action. Understand what that action is. Assist it. Pick up the tempo at which they're moving. Get in step. Find out what kind of economic structure they're building. With their own mud and straw, help them make bricks. If dollars can help, build into every one a safeguard against inflation. Make sure they get down and stay down where they belong— with the people. Talk in the people's language. Avoid giving charity and gifts. Be as ready to learn as to teach. Don't be surprised if, in the end, you get more than you give. Above all, don't think America can win Asia with dollars. Only Asians can build a free, democratic Asia. America can only help."

Back in Bekonan, the *lurah* put it more simply. *"Gotong rojong,"* he said. "Let us do it together."

EIGHT

"Red Is Our Emblem"

N OT IN A LONG TIME had anything stirred Solo's teen-agers so much as the presence in their midst of a flesh-and-blood American family. Almost from the day of our arrival we noticed boys and girls of high-school age staring at us from the street, and we wondered how we could make them know they were welcome. Jill and Arthur, luckily, suffered from none of the clumsy self-consciousness that poisons adult efforts to ingratiate themselves with young people. Utterly innocent of political, racial and other divisive tensions, guileless in manner, and with no palpable purpose other than to make friends for friendship's sake, they talked and laughed with them, took their hands and drew them to our porch, where Eadie kept an ice locker filled with Dutch water. The number of visitors grew until more than a score of boys and girls overflowed our porch and garden every afternoon. It was gratifying and, we thought, significant, that none of Asia's proclaimed attitudes toward the United States extended to Americans as individuals. They called Eadie *Bu,* or Mom, and me *Pak,* or Dad, adopted Arthur and Jill as brother and sister, and never stopped asking how they could achieve their life's ambition—a visit to America.

We quickly discovered that their visits stemmed from more

than friendship and curiosity. All were high-school students who were studying English, chosen by Indonesia's Parliament as the first foreign language of the land. Deadly serious about mastering its grammar and pronunciation, they brought along dog-eared copies of Hollywood magazines and horror comics and took turns reading aloud.

Murder was Lefty's job. He ran it like a business. Somebody wanted somebody else rubbed out and you just put in a call for Lefty. His fee varied from one grand to five thousand. It all depended on how big the pigeon was. Lefty had no scruples about killing anybody. The guy had to die—Lefty got the job, cased him and then pulled the trigger.

Eadie bore the brunt of the task of unraveling idioms, reducing slang to dictionary terms and explaining meanings. She also pointed out that their choice of literature was hardly representative of America's best, and that it was descriptive of but a small fraction of our national life.

"But, *Bu,*" a student protested, "if there are better books in America, why do you send us only these?"

"*Bu,*" said another, "we see these same things in American movies. If life in America is different, why wouldn't your books and movies show it?"

In that early stage of our sojourn in Solo, neither Eadie nor I could answer their questions. Instead, we vainly searched the bookstalls for something that did America more justice. We also waited for the arrival of a moving picture about which we could say, "Be sure to see it. It shows America as it really is." It never came. Meanwhile Eadie bought the few available tattered copies of the *Reader's Digest,* the only quasi-serious American publication to be found among the crime, sex and horror

87

paperbacks displayed in the stalls. As sensitively edited for foreign as for popular American tastes, the *Digests* became prime favorites with our group. Pending better knowledge of the book and movie situation, Eadie depended on daily readings from the *Digests,* plus maximum exposure to our own family's unsensational behavior, to put America in better perspective. She also managed to shift the conversation to the students themselves, their lives, difficulties, ambitions. This tactic not only gave us time to grasp the problem of America's self-projection to Indonesia, but also furnished insight into that crucially important segment of Indonesia's youth—those who, by dint of good fortune or sheer ability, were climbing the educational ladder to key roles in their country's future.

About half the group were sons and daughters of better-off families—merchants, professionals, landowners and officials who lived in Solo, close to the secondary schools—to whom opportunities for higher education came rather easily. The others, children of farmers and workers, had shown better-than-average ability in elementary school; their families were making incalculable sacrifices to give them their chance. Among their countless kin, including one or two, perhaps, who were well heeled, money was raised not only for clothes, food, tuition and textbooks, but also to enable the fathers and mothers to get along without the services of the absent child. Eadie and I were deeply impressed by the students' willingness to give up their afternoons, day after day, to practice English, to learn about America, and to discuss themselves and their country in a serious vein.

We were also astonished by the broad range of their interests. Eadie never knew whether she would be asked about Woodrow Wilson and why America had refused to join the League of Nations, or about the correct way to manage a knife and fork. Nor were their questions altogether innocent. One day they hammered away at America's treatment of Negroes. Next day they talked about our Indians, asserting a knowledge of alleged discriminatory practices which exceeded our own. The third day the cat crept out of the bag. Their queries had been prompted by a debate raging between the Communist and non-Communist factions in their school. The Communists, that morning, had posed a clincher: Would Eadie and I be as hospitable to them back home in America as we were in Solo? Or would we shun them as outcasts, as other colored peoples visiting in the United States were shunned? They recited a long list of humiliations suffered by Orientals in American airports and restaurants.

Eadie said her home was wherever we and the children happened to be, and that it was always open to people we liked and respected, regardless of race. This she could prove only when and if they came to America. Meanwhile, the Communists were welcome to join our afternoon meetings and raise their questions themselves instead of using the others as cat's-paws. The next day's session was swelled by three lads and two girls representing the Communist faction. Suspicious and a little sullen at first, they rapidly warmed and talked as freely as the others. The only discernible difference was that whereas the rest of the group had large repertoires of American song hits, which they loved to sing, and kept scrapbooks of American film stars, the Communists disdained such decadent nonsense.

Their leader was Atmo, a lissome youth of almost feminine gracefulness, whose liquid eyes and white smile illuminated an otherwise somber manner. Over the months, we formed a deep attachment to the boy, who, little by little, revealed the background which shaped his political views. Though young, he clearly remembered colonial times. "I can never forget my grandfather's discouragement," he said. "He was a clerk in the post office. Whenever an opening occurred higher up, a Dutchman would fill it. For the same work he did, a white man half his age received higher pay. When he complained, the official in charge said a white man could not live like a Javanese. 'You are barefoot, like apes. Apes can't speak Dutch and neither can you. For you, two cents a day is ample.'

"One day my father took me all the way to Malang to a new swimming pool the Dutch had built. Outside was a sign, 'No dogs or natives allowed.' He took me instead to the amusement park. There were two entrances, one for the whites and one for us. My father told me to address the Dutch as *Tuan Besar*, Great Master. Behind their backs we called them Drunks, Loud-Mouthed Boors, Impolite Ones. Between us and the white children there was war. They formed the A-I, or anti-native club, and beat up any of us they thought too cocky. We organized *pentjak* clubs and fought them on the streets. The police arrested us and let them go. In the courts, justice always favored the whites. At an early age we learned our fathers' way was best—to oppose them quietly, living two lives—a peaceful life they could see, and a life of vengeance we hid from them.

"We took our revenge in little ways, such as when a fat Dutch official asked me what I ate at home. I said *telek lendung*, slang for chicken manure. He had never heard of it. I told him it was a bird that flew only at night. 'Very interesting,' he said, smacking his lips. 'I shall ask my cook to prepare one for my dinner.'

"To the West," said Atmo, "colonialism is a political abstraction, to be solved by diplomats. To us, colonialism is the memory of humiliations so deep that even now, when we are free, I wake up at night sweating with shame and resentment."

Everyone in the group had shared Atmo's experience with colonialism and was as marked by it. Eadie asked if there had been a more pleasant side to their childhood. Their faces lighted up as they reminisced about soccer games, kite-flying and *nini-dok*, the most Javanese of their pastimes.

"On a night when the moon was full," said one of the girls, "preferably on a Thursday night when the spirits would not let us sleep, we would build a doll out of rice stalks and bury it for half an hour in some holy place, like a cemetery, or under a waringin tree. Then we would dig it up, carry it to the village and form a circle around it, each child pulling a string attached to the figure to make it dance. We'd sing a magic song:

> *Wake up little rice plants, wake up.*
> *You are turning green,*
> *Green as a new bride.*
> *Shepherd, shepherd, climb that blimbing tree,*
> *Even though it is slippery.*
> *Climb up and wash the bridegroom's clothes.*

"Then, one by one, we'd drop the strings. The doll would continue to dance alone. When it fell down, the game was over."

Eadie asked how many of these high-school students believed that the doll really danced by itself. All raised their hands. Atmo said, "My little brother plays *ninidok* with his friends. He believes it too. We all do."

They talked of other happy memories, of pigeons with whistles in their tails, cooing doves, and lizards living in the rafters that croaked *tokay, tokay, tokay* until they were breathless. As children, they listened at night and, with the croaks, said,

"Rich-poor, rich-poor," hoping the last croak would come out on "rich."

"To be sure," said Atmo, "I said, 'Rich, rich, rich,' because I yearned to live in a fine house and own a motorcycle. These, of course, were only for the whites. If we were ever to have such things, we knew we must rely on cleverness. This was the moral underlying all our legends and history. The first story my mother told me was about a goat and a rabbit who came upon a stone post set in the ground. They challenged each other to move it. The goat butted it with all his strength and merely broke his horns. The rabbit burrowed the earth around the post and toppled it over."

Eadie was curious about the heroes they venerated. Preeminent were the wajang princes, especially Arjuna, brave, handsome, clever, husband and lover of hundreds of beautiful women. Another great wajang hero was Bima, man of action, bravest of soldiers. Kresno, adviser to the princes, was admired as one able to outwit his enemies, and for his understanding of life.

Atmo related the most moving and significant, to him, of the wajang's episodes. "Arjuna, driven from his kingdom by his half-brothers, the evil Kurawas, asked Kresno: 'Is it good to win back a kingdom if, to do so, I must kill my blood brothers? I would rather be a beggar than the murderer of my kin.' Kresno answered: 'You are wrong. In making such a choice you exalt your own self and place your feelings above all else. The highest morality is to lose your personality, to submerge yourself as an individual, to detach yourself from your actions. Kill your own family, but kill without passion.'"

Other heroes came from Indonesian history. Outstanding was Ken Angrok, a poor farm boy who became a thief and then a soldier in the Regent's army. Ordered to seize his former bandit friends, he obeyed, but he begged the Regent to spare them. The Regent agreed, and Ken Angrok, after converting the thieves into soldiers, was promoted to the rank of commander. He immediately murdered the Regent and mounted the throne.

Ken Angrok was murdered in turn, and Kertanagara, another great hero, seized power. When Chinese ambassadors arrived at his palace to demand that he make a pilgrimage to Peiping and pay homage to Kublai Khan, Kertanagara mutilated them and sent them back with his refusal. Kublai Khan dispatched an army to attack him, but, before it landed, Kertanagara himself was assassinated and his kingdom was divided. His son-in-law, Widjaja, submitted to the new king but cleverly tricked him into granting him a domain which he built into the new kingdom of Madjapahit. When the Chinese came, he allied himself with them and defeated his benefactor. Then he turned on the Chinese and drove them out of Java.

Treachery and guile, it seemed, were the qualities Atmo most admired in Indonesia's heroes. The exception was Diponegoro, who trounced the Dutch fairly in battle after battle. The Dutch commander, De Kock, finally invited Diponegoro to a peace conference, promising that no harm would befall him during the negotiations. "Diponegoro," said Atmo, "made the mistake of believing De Kock. He was seized and exiled. De Kock's deceit is something no Indonesian can ever forget. We would be fools to be taken in again by a white man's promises."

Atmo clearly remembered much that happened when the Second World War broke over Java. "Radio Tokyo began broadcasting to Indonesia. The headman of our village had a hidden receiver. Every night at nine the program started with 'Indonesia Raja,' our national anthem, banned by the Dutch.

Then a voice would speak. 'Indonesians! Do not despair! The hour of your liberation is near! The Japanese army is coming to set you free!'

"When the Japanese arrived, the colonialists collapsed like bags of wind. They gave all kinds of excuses: 'The British and Americans have let us down. We can't fight alone.' Suddenly we realized white men could be beaten by Asians. Our joy in being free was marred only by the realization that we had been fooled for centuries. We hailed the Japanese as our saviors. They banished the Dutch language and marched the *belandas* off to barbed-wire cages. The symbols the Dutch had painted on the walls, 'V, V, V for Victory,' turned upside down, became 'A, A, A—Asia, Asia, Asia!'

"Our happiness lasted two weeks. Then everything changed. Welcoming committees were jailed and tortured by the Kempi-tei to force out hidden wealth. It was left behind by the Dutch, they said, for guerrilla warfare. Farmhouses and granaries were raided, and rice was carted away to feed their troops. Forced agriculture was restored; we were told exactly what to plant. If you didn't do what they ordered, you were tortured or killed.

"Males between fourteen and twenty-five were marched off for military training and disappeared into the Hei Ho, the auxiliary army corps, or the Peta, a so-called Indonesian army, or the Romusha, the slave-labor corps. In every village the Jawa Hokokai, the propaganda organization, showed moving pictures of Japanese victories. Again and again we were forced to see *Indonesia Raja,* a beautiful film showing our countryside and our children, filled with joy at their new freedom, with the Hei Ho and Peta marching happily into battle. Ah, what a lovely film that was. And what a lie!

"The Japs overlooked nothing. They moved our clocks to Tokyo time, our calendars to 2602. Every morning we bowed toward the Emperor, swearing to work for the victory of Asia. We sang a song called 'Destroy our Enemies.'

> *Beware of the Englishmen and the Americans.*
> *They are the enemies of the world.*
> *They want to make us slaves of their desire.*
> *Destroy our enemies.*
> *They are Englishmen and Americans.*

"How we hated Japs! We called them 'Little Cocks.' They forced us to shout *Dai Nippon Banzai!* We changed *banzai* to *bangsat,* or bandit. They never discovered that we were shouting 'The Japs are bandits!' One thing kept our hopes alive— the ancient prophecy of King Djojobojo, that after three hundred years of white man's rule, a yellow race from the north would drive out the whites. They would remain as long as it takes corn to grow between planting and harvest. Then Indonesia would be free. It turned out that three months meant three years. In the end, the prophecy came true.

"But nothing in life is all bad. The Japs left us some good things too. We learned to run things the Dutch had never entrusted to us—trains, the post office, typewriters, telephones. That gave us confidence in ourselves we had never had before. And Javanese religious and patriotic organizations set up schools. For the first time, in the villages, kids like us could get an education.

"Also, we learned never to trust propaganda. We were forced to obey their orders before the cameras. Then we would see ourselves in the pictures, singing and cheering happily for the Emperor. It was a lie—our smiling faces hid tears and groans of shame."

I couldn't resist asking, "Are you sure of that, Atmo? May

not the things you believe about the perfection of life in Russia and China also be propaganda?" Atmo shook his head. "No. Too many have been there and seen what life is like. What one sees with one's own eyes is not propaganda."

All the youngsters in the group vividly recalled the end of the war, the beginning of the revolution. In Atmo's words:

"On August 17, 1945, the Japanese seemed nervous and sad. That day they paid little heed to their work. Since newspapers and radio were censored, we didn't know why. We didn't know Japan had surrendered. Suddenly a broadcast from Djakarta brought exciting news. We had no radio and did not hear it. But one magic word, *Merdeka!*—Independence!—spread from mouth to mouth until everyone knew. We were free!

" 'We, the people of Indonesia, herewith proclaim the independence of Indonesia.' These were the exact words uttered by Sukarno and Hatta. We set up representatives to take over power from the Japanese, and to manage local affairs. Many of the older men were members of the Keibodan, the people's defense corps set up by the Japs, and armed with bamboo spears. We boys belonged to the Seinendan, scout groups trained by the Japs to fight. Together we marched up to the Japs and demanded their guns. Some of them haggled, but they soon gave in. One garrison in Semarang, the Kidobutai, made up of suicide troops, refused to surrender and killed some Indonesian civilians. We all drove down to the city and attacked. We were only nine- or ten-year-olds, but we had our first taste of battle. It lasted five days. Then the English came and there was a cease-fire. In the night, we stole the guns and retired.

"We learned the magic power of rifles and machine guns. Each of us felt like Arjuna or Bima. We banded together into companies, with names like Bamboo Spikes or Alapalaps (Harriers). I joined the Srikandi troop. My sister joined the Lasjwi,

96

the girls' brigade. Our army was called the People's Safety
Corps. When the Dutch raised their flag before the Orange
Hotel, we rushed to the road, climbed aboard trucks, oxcarts,
anything going to Surabaja. We had no strategy, no tactics. All
we had was our war cry, *Bersiap!*—Be ready! Whenever we
heard it, we killed the nearest Dutchman, Englishman or any
other *belanda* we could reach.

"Then Sukarno announced the formation of political parties.
Quarrels broke out among us. Our Srikandi troop disbanded.
Some of us joined the Hisbullah (Hope of God), the Masjumi
Army. Some joined the Buffalo Army of the Nationalists; others
the Pesindo, the Socialist Youth Army.

"The Pesindo's flag was red, with a white star. Amir Sjari-
fuddin was the leader. He was a Communist. He told us communism meant *merdeka*. Communism meant equality—no more
bowing to Dutchmen, rajahs, sultans or anyone else. *Merdeka*
was what I wanted. I joined the Communists and tied a red
scarf around my neck. We sang:

> *Red is our emblem.*
> *Red means courage.*
> *The star means equality.*
> *That is our emblem.*
> *That is our emblem.*"

At first, the boys and girls had blindly followed their individual leaders into different political camps. Ideologically, the
differences among them were too small for children to understand. Then, in 1948, at the moment of the young Republic's
greatest peril, with Dutch armies surrounding Sukarno's government, the Communists had plunged a dagger in its back at
Madiun. The revolt was quelled and the Communists' intent

97

betrayed. Thousands ripped off their Pesindo insignia and renounced their Communist oaths. Atmo and his Communist friends admitted that for a time their own faith had been shaken.

"What restored it?" Eadie asked.

Atmo replied, "My leader reminded us of Bima's advice to Arjuna: 'The highest morality is to lose your personality, to submerge yourself as an individual, to detach yourself from your actions. Kill your own family, but kill without passion.' "

NINE

"Out of Many, One"

UNWILLING TO LET our home become an arena of political strife, Eadie managed, in the following weeks, to switch the youngsters' talk to education. One way or another, despite war, occupation and revolution, these youngsters had managed to complete six years in the elementary schools established by Javanese religious and patriotic organizations after the defeat of the Dutch. Atmo's experience differed little from the others, but certain overtones and developments gave it, for us, more than average interest.

His grades were high and he was eligible for one of the six secondary schools set up in Solo. When his father was offered a post as chemistry teacher in the high school, the family moved to the city. Atmo kept meticulous notebooks, and we were struck by these descriptions of the Soviet Union and the United States, excerpted from his geography textbooks:

In Europe there is only one country larger than Indonesia. That is Russia. And there is only one country with greater population density—Russia. Russia is the first country of Europe. It consists of two parts, one in Europe, the other in Asia. The bigger part of Russia lies in our continent. All the land is owned by the government.

Farmers have proprietary rights to use the land. Russian agriculture is mostly mechanized. This means that all work is done with the help of machines—plowing, sowing, reaping, etc. There are more than 700,000 agricultural machines in Russia. They are manufactured by the metal industries, which also produce trucks, airplanes, trains, weapons and munitions. All these factories and mines belong to the state.

Russia consists of many republics bound together in a union, the Union of the Soviet Socialist Republics. In this union, farmers and workers hold all power.

America is five times larger than Indonesia, with 150 million people. One tenth are Negroes. They live in the South and plant cotton and corn. White men do everything else. They run the factories and the government. How rich America is! It produces 70 per cent of the world's petroleum, 45 per cent of its steel, 40 per cent of its coal, 40 per cent of its aluminum. Because of its riches, the U.S.A. became the most industrial area in the world. What does one think of when one hears names like these: Douglas, Chevrolet, Singer, Ford, Kodak? These are the corporations that rule America.

With other bright students, Atmo, after three years of secondary school, entered the public high school. Solo boasted five such schools, with a total enrollment of about four thousand. Atmo paid thirty-five cents a month for tuition. Boys and girls below the public school's standards could enter one of the twenty-four private schools, which charged a dollar and twenty-five cents a month. Even at this relatively high cost, the schools enrolled another eight thousand students from families in higher income brackets. High school curricula included advanced algebra and geometry, physics, commercial knowledge, chemistry, government and English. I was especially interested in how the last three were taught, and so I accepted Atmo's invitation to visit his school.

It was an imposing building built around a playground. A commodious parking space was filled with students' bicycles. Posters in the entrance hall advertised soccer, art, debating and music competitions sponsored by Porksla, the Indonesian High School Association for Sport and Art. A library listed two hundred books, eleven in English. Between classes, students strolled and chatted or studied under the trees. The modern, Western character of the place was accented by the short bobs and permanents affected by the girls, and the sport shirts and slacks of the boys.

The government class was held in a small amphitheater. From a platform the teacher energetically lectured on the spiritual, moral and ethical foundation of the Indonesian state.

"Every country," he said, "is based on ideals which spring from the inner convictions and way of life of its people. The U.S.A. believes in big business, in money, in capitalism. And so its government is one which does all it can to help businessmen manufacture more and more things, so they can get richer and richer. The inner philosophy of the United States is money.

"In the Soviet Union they share another philosophy—that the state itself is supreme and the people exist to serve the state. And so, in Russia, the state owns land and factories and everything else, holding it in trust for the people. In Russia, the state stands even above God and does all it can to make people believe that God does not exist.

"But here in Indonesia, our life and government are not built on such ideals as money and the state-above-God. We have our own philosophy of government and life that serves as our guide in all matters, domestic and foreign. It consists, first, of belief in God—belief in His omnipotent power, to which

101

we as men are subservient. Also, complete freedom for each of us to worship as he pleases. In this we differ from Russia.

"Second, humanism—the belief that men everywhere are more important than machinery, that man's welfare and happiness mean more than money, profits, goods. In this we differ from the United States.

"Third, nationalism—the whole people united in their determination to be free and independent, following our own course, and never becoming a pawn in international politics and wars. We must maintain our right to decide our own attitude and achieve our own aim, a fully independent Indonesia. In this we differ from all countries that would try to make us pawns in their bid for power.

"Fourth, democracy—the belief that the people are supreme and have the right to be governed by men of their own choosing. In this we differ from both Russia and the U.S.A. where, in one, the state rules the people, and, in the other, the people's will is subservient to political bosses and big corporations.

"Fifth, social justice—the belief that all men are equal, entitled to full respect, regardless of color, race or creed, and deserve to share equally in the nation's wealth. In this we differ from America, where there are the very rich and the very poor, and where a Negro has no rights.

"These five principles," concluded the teacher, "are the guiding spirit in our struggle for independence. To them we owe victory over the Dutch, our growing strength, our high moral position in the councils of the world. Our slogan is the message of the wajang, 'Out of many, one.' Arjuna stands for thought and will. Bima, for conscience. Yudhisthira, for holiness. Nakula and Sahadewa stand for desire. Drupadi, the wife of all, for spirit. These senses stand together and cannot be separated.

102

Six is one, and one is six. *Bhinneka tunggal ika!* 'Out of many, one!' "

In the chemistry class, Atmo's father, a slender, suave man, hardly older in appearance than his son, stood at the blackboard and worked out the day's experiments in a series of sketches drawn in chalk. The students copied these in their notebooks. No test tubes, reagents or other equipment common to chemistry laboratories were in evidence. After class I commented on the difficulties of teaching chemistry under such conditions. The teacher nodded.

"But does it not strike you as odd," he asked, "that while our youth are denied the simple materials needed to study science, the foreign corporations spare no expense in extracting and refining our oil with the latest devices? Is it not clear that, for all their pretense, they have no intention of letting Indonesians catch up with their lead in science? Otherwise, here in the high schools is where they would begin. Perhaps it is just as well, for what I lack to teach physical sciences is more than made up by the abundance of examples in the social and political sciences. Few of my students leave my classes without knowing that foreign exploiters of our wealth are blocking their careers. The Indonesian Teachers' Union will not rest until this injustice is wiped out."

Most of Indonesia's teachers, I learned, were union members and readers of its monthly, *Suara Guru,* "Teacher's Voice." Atmo's father checked two articles in the current issue he thought I should see. One was entitled "Today's Indonesian Student."

Today's youth present grave problems which must be solved by the government. If the new generations are to replace the old, they must feel a sense of responsibility to society. To inculcate such a

103

sense, the government has founded many schools and colleges so that young men may train for tasks indispensable to the nation's welfare. That is the design—but what is the reality?

During the revolution students were ready for any sacrifice. Now students think only of themselves. They are disappointed with their lot. They lag behind. Unless a change occurs, they will be gangsters. Moving pictures are influencing our youth and keeping them from school. Many students are working while they study, and they are missing much of what they should be getting from school. Luxury articles, so numerous in Indonesia, distract them and fill them with desire. All this is profitable for the West, where these things come from. It is unfortunate for us, after centuries of colonialism.

The second article was headed "Discrimination against Negroes in the U.S.A."

In the northern states of the U.S.A., mixed marriages sometimes occur. To stir up the white people of the southern states, no better way can be found than to point to these marriages as proof that Negroes may now take white women as wives. Many adult half-breeds, born out of wedlock and unwanted by their fathers, return to live with their black mothers. In southern states and in some northern states too, mixed marriages are forbidden by law. The prohibition of sexual intercourse between Negroes and white men results from the fear that white women will otherwise be without protection. To prevent mixed marriages, these rules prevail:

1. White people must mix less with Negroes.
2. Negroes must be denied all social rights.
3. Negroes and whites must be segregated in schools, churches, shops and other places.

The situation of the Negro woman is worse than tragic. The white man can do with her whatever he wills, and the law does not protect her. A Negro woman, raped by a white man, cannot receive compensation. Should a Negro ravish a white woman, he is thrown into jail and lynched.

Shortly after my visit, annual examinations loomed. Attendance at our soirees fell off. The few lads who came talked of nothing but the importance of the impending tests. Failure meant the end of years of sacrifice and effort, the frustration of all their hopes. An incident occurred at this time which underscored the importance Indonesia's youth attached to education. Two teen-age boys, both former guerrillas and neither a member of our group, began a watch over the cottage adjoining ours. Night and day they spelled each other, never for a moment relaxing their vigilance. One day they drew pistols from their pockets and cleaned them with great ostentation. We became alarmed and asked Samiek to learn why they were there. He reported that the lads were high-school students who were threatening to kill their teacher if they failed the examinations. The man had fled his home, which was in an unprotected kampong and had taken refuge next door. The boys had found him and had renewed their threats and their vigil. Eadie kept the children indoors, out of the line of fire, until one night an ambulance arrived and the teacher was smuggled out on a stretcher.

There was joy in our own group when the results of the examinations were posted. All had passed, and the road to the universities lay open. Talk revolved around careers. Most leaned toward law, the social sciences and the humanities. Out of twenty, only three chose agriculture, medicine and engineering. Then a student arrived one morning and ended our jubilation. He said that Atmo had been arrested for forging a school certificate. He was being tried that afternoon.

The courtroom, when I arrived, was filled with Atmo's class-mates. The judge, gowned in black, entered and took his place on the center of a dais. To his right sat the prosecutor, to his left the clerk. Below the dais was a bench for the accused and other seating accommodations for witnesses and attorneys. After several petty larcenists had been tried, the clerk called Atmo's name. Flanked by a policeman, he entered and bowed to the judge. The marshal held a copy of the Koran over Atmo's head and asked him to repeat: "I will tell the truth in the name of Allah and His Prophet."

The prosecutor read the charges: Atmo had forged and sold high-school diplomas. The judge held up copies of the evidence and asked Atmo if they were his work. Atmo admitted his guilt. He said that after taking his English examinations, he was un-sure of the result. Fearing that after all his hard work he faced failure in this one subject, he had forged the certificate. He had sold copies to friends who, like himself, could not bear the idea of being cut off from the university education to which, all their lives, they had aspired.

An official of the Examination Board pronounced the certifi-cate a forgery and said many like it were in circulation. It was a matter of great concern to the Ministry of Education. Atmo's lawyer begged for clemency on the grounds of the boy's youth and his hitherto excellent record. He said that, since the forger-ies were in the court's hands, the danger was over and a heavy penalty unnecessary. The prosecutor disagreed. He demanded a sentence of nine months in jail.

The judge ordered the courtroom cleared while he conferred with the prosecutor. When the court was reconvened, he ad-dressed Atmo: "In forging and selling certificates, you have harmed all students with bonafide certificates and have contrib-uted to one of the greatest problems facing our country, namely, false admission to higher schools. Only an example will discourage others from committing this crime. I sentence you to nine months in prison."

In the corridor, I met Atmo's father and tried to express my sorrow. "If it had not been for English," he said, "my son might some day have been a Bachelor of Law, instead of a criminal. Whatever we get from your country, even its language, brings with it misfortune."

He turned and, looking suddenly older than the last time I had seen him, walked away.

TEN

"America's Unpardonable Errors in Asia"

FOR YEARS, as a consultant to the Department of State and the United States Information Agency, I had joined in the baffling search for a wave length to Asian hearts and minds—some means, understandable and welcome to Asians, of communicating to them the meaning of America, its cultural, political and economic institutions. Here in Indonesia, I found that two broad, deep channels directly into the main stream of an Asian people's life had been opened to us by the Indonesians themselves. One, of course, was the act of Indonesia's Parliament in naming English as the first foreign language to be taught in the public schools. The other was America's near-monopoly on the moving picture. The undertone of anti-Americanism in the schools, in textbooks and lectures, in the Teachers' Union, made me especially curious to see how these opportunities were being used.

"Imagine," as the principal of one of the local high schools put it, "what might have happened had Russian, not English, been chosen—the flood of cheap textbooks, dictionaries, novels,

108

plays, cultural magazines and movies from Moscow! Imagine the effect of having all lectures in our high schools and universities delivered in two tongues—our own and Russian! Imagine the impact on our youth, our workers, our intellectual elite! Imagine America's outrage that such a one-way street should be opened to communism. Yet it was precisely this opportunity which we granted the English-speaking peoples. Observe, in your daily life among us, the result."

Sitting in the English classrooms in the high school, I listened to students conscientiously imitating the errors of their teachers, who, except in movies, had never heard the language they taught. "How helpful it would be," said one of these teachers—in Indonesian, for his English and mine bore no audible relationship—"if only we had a few phonograph records that pronounced English words and phrases slowly and distinctly. If even I, their teacher, cannot converse with you, what disappointment faces my pupils!"

"Why do you want to master English?" I asked several pupils. "Because we want to build a modern nation," was a common reply. "English is the tool we need to master science, government, economics. It is the most practical of languages." These serious teen-agers then showed me their old-fashioned texts and painfully read from the pages:

The man thrashed the child.
Rich but stupid people.
It often rains in the rainy season.
Damn it! Dash it! Blast it! Curse it! Hang it!

Starting with fairy tales, such as "The Sleeping Beauty," these seekers of practical knowledge advanced to the standard English reader, *Miscellany*. Consisting of thirty-seven excerpts from all English literature, it offered a mutilated version of Shylock's consent to Antonio's request for a loan of money, on the condition that payment be made, if not in kind, with a pound of flesh. From Dickens came the scene in which Oliver Twist, desperate with hunger, asks, "Please, sir, may I have some more?" and takes a thrashing for his recklessness. These classics excepted, most other excerpts came from contemporary American best sellers, such as *Forever Amber,* and oddly selected bits from articles by popular writers, such as "The Noiseless Flash," adapted from John Hersey's famous *Hiroshima.** The last-named began:

On Monday, August 6, 1945, a new era in human history opened. After years of extensive research and experiment, conducted in their latter stages mainly in America, by scientists of many nationalities . . . the forces which hold together the constituent particles of the atom had at last been harnessed to man's use, and on that day man used them. By a decision of America's military authorities, made, it is said, in defiance of the protests of many of the scientists who had worked on the project, an atomic bomb was dropped on Hiroshima. As a direct result, some 60,000 Japanese men, women and children were killed, and almost the whole of a great seaport, a city of 250,000 people, was destroyed by blast and fire.

Contrasting with this account of American brutality was an unattributed article entitled "The Sowjet Union."

In (Russia's) villages, before the Revolution, lived nine-tenths of the Russians, isolated from one another and from the cities, uncon-

* *Hiroshima,* by John Hersey, published by Alfred A. Knopf, Inc.

nected by railroads, telephones or telegraph. Since 1917, vast changes have come over the Russian countryside. Though there are still tens of thousands of log cabin villages, few lack good roads, fewer still have no telephone or telegraph communications, and none are without radio. . . . By 1931, six and a half million peasant households in European Russia had been persuaded to put their little farms, animals and implements into a common pool. Fences and other barriers between separate plots were destroyed, making vast open fields on which tractors and other farm machinery could operate. Statistics show that this social revolution and mechanization have resulted in heavier yields than in Tsarist Russia; certainly the life of the peasants has been raised to a new high level.

The collective farm has brought a bigger population and more social life to the countryside. Every big collective farm has its own theater (with traveling companies of players and their own amateur efforts to fill the bill), cinema and lecture hall, club rooms and library. Some farms produce their own newspaper and are engaged in many cultural activities. Schools, of course, are to be found now everywhere in Russia. As late as 1920 sixty-three out of every hundred people in all Russia were unable to read or write. The education of this tremendous illiterate peasantry must always be the proudest achievement of the Sowjet regime.

Our search for books and magazines which presented America more truthfully ended in failure. The United States Information Service, I knew, maintained excellent libraries, but these served only the three largest cities, hundreds of miles away. Later, in response to my appeal, arrangements were made to ship in book parcels; now little from their storerooms had found their way into villages or towns such as Solo. Instead, in the official Ministry of Information Reading Room, on the main street, readers satisfied their craving for English with copies of

New Times, published in Moscow, and *People's China,* from Peiping.

The few old copies of *Time, Life* and *Reader's Digest* that turned up now and then in bookstalls vanished almost as quickly as they appeared. Why, I asked the proprietors, did they carry so few decent, serious American publications?

"And where would I find them?" one merchant asked. "I am glad to get whatever old papers my Chinese wholesaler can scrape up from the cities' trash. When they are sold, months may pass before I am lucky enough to come across another bundle. As for new books and magazines from America, who could afford to buy them? A man can feed his family for a month for the price of one American book."

Our own few volumes were in constant demand. One day, when the editor of the town's newspaper came to return a borrowed book, he seemed loath to replace it on our shelf. "How I would love to own a few American books! Why isn't it possible for me to buy them for the few rupiahs I can afford?"

I mentioned my talk with the bookdealers. "The problem of distributing American books cheaply seems just too difficult to overcome."

The editor seized my arm and strode down the street to a Chinese grocery. Pointing to a glistening red-and-white machine, flanked by boxes of empty bottles, he said, "America can manufacture and export this complicated machine. America can supply the bottles, the caps, the sweet syrup, the soda water. America can fill the bottles, chill them to exactly the right temperature and sell them in this town for about five American pennies. Allah alone knows the problems involved, but American genius solved them. But books that might teach us how your country started as a colony, like ours, and learned how to govern itself in freedom—books that might inspire our people to work and save and become rich like yours—such books present problems the American brain cannot solve. Can it be that in books there are no profits, and that unless there are profits Americans don't care?"

I argued stubbornly that books involved authors, royalties, international copyright laws, other problems the soft-drink industry apparently escaped. He remained unconvinced. Back at our house, we found the usual group of youngsters, this time gathered to serenade us with a new medley of American songs.

> *Darling, why do I get butterflies*
> *Every time I'm kissing you?*
> *When you hold me tight and close your eyes*
> *Do you get butterflies too?*

Upon the editor's request, one of the lads handed him a copy of a little booklet entitled *Fascinating Rhythm*. Embellished with a rear view of the most titillating of America's current crop of actresses, and captioned "Hey Hey Sex Looking!" it contained twenty erotic lyrics with ukulele accompaniment. I recognized it as just one of dozens of similar publications widely available in every fair-sized Javanese village for about five cents. The editor dropped it on our bookshelf, alongside our expensive, hard-cover volumes, smiled at us wryly, and left.

At Gadja Mada, one of Indonesia's three universities, the white-haired president added a new dimension to the problem.

"There are about thirty thousand university students in Indonesia. They face grave difficulties, not the least of which is the need for mastering English. Only about thirty per cent of those entering Gadja Mada graduate. Some take nine years to complete a five-year course, often because their command of English is faulty. But those who succeed are very special people. They

113

are the future leaders of Indonesia—our engineers, doctors, teachers, Cabinet ministers. What they learn here may forge their attitude and outlook—and Indonesia's—forever.

"America has a unique chance to influence this crucial group, for English is our self-chosen avenue to Western knowledge. But America has failed us completely. We receive catalogues from American publishers. Sometimes we receive one or two copies of a certain title—enough to whet our appetites. Many of the titles we recognize as the best in the field. But we do not have the dollars to pay for them. USIS has helped us with medical books. But in economics, sociology, pedagogy, law—in all other critically important fields in which we seek to learn from America—we must fall back on Dutch or German or any other texts we can afford. Many Americans visit us and promise to help us get the books we need. Then they leave and forget us. We think Americans lack *bona fides*—good faith."

I talked to undergraduates in dormitories and on the campus. They poured out their bitterness. "Often our only hope of passing a course is to study the American texts. Two or three books may exist—one under glass in the library, another on the professor's desk, a third for perhaps two hundred students. It is hopeless! We welcomed English as a doorway to a better future, for our country and ourselves. Instead, it has become a barrier. The only place where we can afford to study English is in the movies. If what they show is all America has to teach us, perhaps it is just as well that we cannot afford your books."

Matching America's near-monopoly on foreign-language instruction in Indonesia's schools was America's hold on Indonesia's theaters. The chief difference was that, whereas books

114

for the literate were scarce, movies for the illiterate masses were everywhere.

Seven films out of every ten shown in Indonesia came from Hollywood. No other form of entertainment—not even the people's beloved but costly live-action shadow plays—matched our films in popularity. As the local representative of a large American studio told me: "There's at least one theater in every town of ten thousand and over. We figure our audience at twenty-five million a week. Even the poorest farmer can afford to treat his family to a movie on holidays, and he does. With a demand like that, we have to scrape the bottom of the barrel to supply the theaters. Pictures we wouldn't look at in the States draw packed houses here. It's a gold mine. They like good pictures best—*Ben Hur* and *Quo Vadis,* for example. But anything goes."

Lurid posters advertising American films emblazoned every Indonesian town. Solo's main street, one day, shrilled with "I Confess," depicting a man embracing a half-nude woman under the caption "Crushed Lips Can't Talk!" Another poster featured: "Bold! Blunt! Brutal! Today's most searching story of youth written in shame and shock, tears and tragedy, truth and terror—MAN CRAZY!" Illustrated was a titian-haired teen-ager in revealing disarray, a cigarette smoking in her lips, a pistol smoking in her hand. A third showed a couple kissing, silhouetted against a United States Air Force bomber. *"Above and Beyond,"* read the caption. "The love story behind the billion-dollar secret." A fourth advertised *"Vicki*—If they want to look at me, let them pay for it!" A fifth, *"Captain Scarlett*—a price on his head . . . a sword in his hand . . . a woman in his arms."

Eadie and I often joined the multitudes packing Solo's seven movie houses. We went because we frankly enjoy movies and have never been among those who, on moral grounds, demand

115

that Hollywood be banished or reformed. But, whereas we could place the violent sexuality and crime flashing across the screen week after week in true perspective, knowing when they touched truth and when they strove for effect by exaggeration, Indonesians came, saw and believed. Here, in flashing Technicolor and stereophonic sound, was America.

Perhaps the best film exhibited in Solo during our stay was *Above and Beyond*. Its kiss-drenched, bomb-in-flight posters did little justice to the theme—the moral dilemma America faced in dropping the first A-bomb on Japan. Love, suspense, other Hollywood clichés were interwoven without banality. It was first-class entertainment. Eadie and I thoroughly enjoyed it. So, we judged, did the rest of the audience. But next day we ran into this reaction: "By itself, *Above and Beyond* would do America credit. But after seeing dozens of pictures about war, bombers, destruction, after reading speeches about massive retaliation, after hearing of your experiments' effects on a Japanese fishing vessel, it becomes just one more proof of your preoccupation with military power. You seem fascinated by your destructive capacities. Why, we wonder, is there not a film about the positive uses of atomic power?"

One evening, after attending a showing of *Flamingo Road* with an Indonesian couple, Eadie was asked, "Does every American town and village have a night club?"

"Of course not," she replied. "In our entire state of New Hampshire, there probably aren't twenty night clubs such as you saw tonight."

"Then where do you gamble and drink?" the husband asked.

"Most of us," I answered, "don't seriously gamble and drink. If we do, it's usually in a friendly way, at home."

The Indonesian shook his head. "But American movies show that *everybody* gambles and drinks in night clubs, and punches women, and carries guns. They prove Americans love violence and war—especially dropping bombs from airplanes."

Eadie struggled to hide her hurt. "I have never carried a gun in my life. There isn't a night club in our New Hampshire village. And if anyone in the world hates war, it's Americans!"

The Indonesian shrugged. "All we know about America we learn from your own movies. We say, 'Americans are either kissing or killing.'" Then came the clincher. "If there were another side to America, why wouldn't you show it in your films?"

Weeks later, after another evening at the movies, Eadie awakened one night and nudged me. "Tell me, was I wrong in telling the Slamets we don't carry guns, or guzzle whisky, or thrill to a good atom bombing? It's so long since we were home, might it be that we've forgotten?"

We continued to enjoy American movies, their vigor, movement and often honest self-criticism. Some of the worst of them were better entertainment than their Russian and Chinese competition. All the same, we could not help concluding that the most successful traducers of their own country, its way of life at home, its aims and actions overseas, were Americans. We achieved heartfelt sympathy for our official Information Agency, which, with its three libraries, its few documentary films and its handful of leaflets, was striving against all manner of obstacles, economic and other, to dilute the poison dispensed by America's misinformation agencies. We lost confidence, finally, in our own ability to dispel the doubts building up in the minds of many of America's best friends in Indonesia—men like the chairman of Indonesia's Cultural Congress, who said:

"Officially, America presents itself to Asia as noble, generous, idealistic. Unofficially, you reveal yourselves as a people debauched by everything that, in our Moslem code, is rotten and vile. Even our illiterate people recognize and reject official

117

propaganda. But they tend to believe your own projection of your country in commercial, unofficial forms. Educated people know your films are for entertainment and do not show America as it really it. But even we cannot understand a country that will sell its own soul by exporting such filth for money. When Communists claim America is decadent and materialistic, what can we say?"

Or a local high-school teacher: "This town was changed overnight by one picture, *Niagara*. The star walked in a strange way, her hips and breasts shaking with every step. After that, you could see girls on our streets showing off their breasts and buttocks. In school, the boys call these girls 'American atom-age women.' For the first time, there is disrespect and evil intercourse between our boys and girls. Therefore, when our Teachers' Union attacks America in our magazine, we believe the worst about you."

Or the president of the local chapter of Perwari, Indonesia's Women's Association: "America seems determined systematically to destroy the culture and values which Eastern women have always cherished. Its temptations are so beguiling, our youth have no defense. They are being set adrift, and in our work with young girls we deal with the consequences. I have friends who have visited your country. They tell me the movies and magazines we see here do not show the real America. If that is so, why do you send these falsehoods to Indonesia? Don't you realize that though they do us great harm, the harm they do America is even greater?"

Bereft of answers, I sought among other Americans further insight into America's exploitation of the opportunities provided by its near-monopoly on movies and foreign-language teaching. A film executive in Djakarta stated his position clearly: "Your friends may say our movies hurt America in

118

Asian eyes. But the box office says the opposite. I have even been told that if Alan Ladd ordered an Asian to fight communism, he'd obey. You can't discount that. Doubtless, in anything as big as the movie business, there may be abuses. Maybe we aren't doing America complete justice. But outside censors aren't going to fix whatever is wrong. The American movie industry is patriotic enough to clean up its own house. I'm confident that if the problem were fairly presented, Hollywood would find the right answers."

Another qualified American, after reading my notes on the movies' effect on Asian audiences, strove hard for a balanced evaluation. He wrote:

I have never been able to reach any firm conclusion in my own mind about the impact of American movies overseas. What struck me as the most penetrating study I saw done while I was in the State Department came to the conclusion—largely subjective, its author would admit—that American movies shocked, annoyed or struck as frivolous or boring pretty much the same types of people overseas that they affect in that way in this country, that these intellectuals and conservatives tended to be the ones that American intellectuals most saw, and that there was a mutual concurrence of their views on the subject. The conclusion further was, however, that American movies were enormously popular—as they obviously are—with the great bulk of people overseas who find the life portrayed in them exciting and desirable, and indeed to be emulated, even if the emulation sometimes takes the pattern of the sexy postures that the Indonesian school teacher disapproved of.

No other nation has ever been even comparably successful in getting hundreds of millions of people abroad to spend hours seeing us as we show ourselves to ourselves. I expect the enormous popularity of American movies underlies the universal conviction

119

abroad that while the United States is popular or unpopular, wise or unwise, courteous or rude, it is at least vast, powerful, and effective; and this in many ways may be a more useful conviction than to be liked. Practically all Germans in 1939 and 1940, I expect, were convinced that the French were cultured, pleasant, civilized, refined, and unaggressive people, but it didn't stop World War II, and if the Japanese had been a little more convinced of American power they might have avoided Pearl Harbor, whereas no amount of convincing the Japanese of our cultural sympathies would have done any good.

We are, after all, a pretty rudely vital people and I don't think are greatly harmed by recognition of the fact. But no matter how favorably you interpret the situation as it is, there is certainly room to make a far superior service of an instrument so powerful that even its present blind and clumsy use is helpful to us.

This letter did not persuade Eadie or me. It seemed to us to evade the basic issue. It overlooked the movies' impact, not on intellectuals, but on Asia's masses.

The director of the Indonesian operations of the Ford Foundation, which almost alone has perceived and responded to the people's need for assistance in learning English, described the situation in his field:

The appetite for English language instruction, at all levels, beggars description. America's answer to this need is thirteen teacher-trainers, ten tape recorders, ten typewriters with phonetic symbols and a few books donated by USIS from its limited supply. My own judgment of our program is that we are failing to meet our opportunity and responsibility. America has the knowledge of audio-visual techniques necessary to make English a useful tool for the students, farmers and workers of this country. We aren't using this knowledge here. It is a task worthy of our great foundations, universities and other private agencies. If only they would co-ordinate their information, methods and funds, they could go far in winning for America Asia's appreciation and trust. Even more, they could actually help mold Asia's newborn institutions in democratic patterns."

No one, it seemed to me, put the case so succinctly as the "Benjamin Franklin" of the young republic—the ancient, bearded Hadji Agus Salim. Said this tiny man, leader of his people's nationalist movement from inception to victory, and affectionately known to them as "Indonesia's Grand Old Man":

"Let me tell you a secret. In 1921, after the Russian Revolution and the Spartacus movement in Germany, two books entitled *Revolutionary Culture* and *Revolutionary Mass Actions* were smuggled into this country. They were passed from hand to hand, from group to group, until thousands of us were inspired with the will and knowledge to be free. We owe our independence to those books. Such is the power of ideas. Today, some of these revolutionary ideas are discredited. We turn for refreshment to America. We choose your language as the means of reading the best of your books. We trample upon each other to pay our few hard-earned rupiahs to see your moving pictures. Perhaps, during your stay among us, you have seen the consequences.

"Your country," concluded the Hadji, "faces many difficulties in Asia. No mortal is wise enough to meet them all without making mistakes, and Allah asks us to forgive. But in its failure to seize these chances to inform us, strengthen us and win us to its side, America has committed unpardonable errors. May you correct them before it is too late."

121

ELEVEN

"The Grand Old Man of Indonesia"

A FEW DAYS after our talk, Indonesia's "Grand Old Man," the Hadji, died. Flags flew at half-mast, and gloom lay thick in the kampongs. Wherever their political loyalties lay, all loved and admired this molecule of a man, less than five feet high, last survivor of the band that, fifty years before, had given Indonesian nationalism the impulse that led to freedom. Organizer of one of the first of his country's political parties, editor, foreign-affairs minister, representative of his people at Mecca and the All-Asian Conference at New Delhi, ambassador to the Arab lands of the Middle East, and pleader for his people's independence at the United Nations, the wise, temperate Hadji well deserved the respect of Indonesians and Dutch alike.

My interview with him was his last. Passing his house, I had seen him, through the window, peering at his newspapers through thick-lensed glasses, stroking his stubby white beard, looking like the incarnation of all Asia's wisdom. He had answered my knock and seemed pleased to have a visitor. I felt as though I had suddenly stumbled on a chance to ask a Jefferson, a Sun Yat-sen, a Gandhi, as he stood on death's threshold, to reveal his last thoughts about his life, his country, his people.

The Hadji spoke English perfectly, but slowly, and I had written down each word as it fell from his tired lips. "Yes," he said, "I am the last of the old guard who has seen the whole revolution. If you sincerely desire to understand our people and country, you must try to understand the nature and course of this revolution. It began in 1911. The Chinese were responsible for it. The Chinese had long lived amongst us, an oppressed race. The men wore pigtails. The women we rarely saw. Suddenly, almost overnight, they became a different people. The men cut off their pigtails, and Chinese women were seen on the streets and in the shops. The reasons were Sun Yat-sen and the revolution in China. A people who for years had been dormant proved they could shake off the past with new, progressive ideas.

"The influence of all this on us was great. The Dutch were impressed too. They permitted the settlement of Chinatowns and the establishment of Chinese schools. Chinese became self-respecting, proud of their nation and race. They developed as tradesmen and wholesalers. The Dutch handled them cautiously and treated them with more consideration than they showed to Indonesians. The lesson was clear: We too had to assert our sense of nationality. We too had to shake off the past and be free. We owe that first impulse to Sun Yat-sen and China. If intellectuals among the Dutch supported us, it was because they knew it was better that Indonesia be led to independence by the Dutch themselves than that Indonesians should win independence despite and against the Dutch. We were well on our way to achieving autonomy when oil was found in Sumatra. Overnight, the discovery changed Indonesia from an agricultural into a strategic oil economy. Indonesia suddenly became important to the West, and Holland became responsible for the maintenance of the law and order that were indispensable to Western exploitation of our oil.

"Now the Dutch were committed to carry the white man's burden. 'The sacred mission of civilization' were their words. Men like Deterding and Colijn of Royal Dutch Shell replaced liberal Dutchmen. They wanted big estates around the oil wells to keep natives away. After oil exploitation began, there was no longer room for compromise between us. 'Get rid of the Dutch' became our slogan. Also, 'Get rid of the oil barons.' And that is another step in understanding Indonesians. Oil cheated us of our early independence. A new dimension was added to our fear and hatred of white men, of big corporations, of capitalism, of Western duplicity and sanctimony.

"Then, in 1918, came the Russian Revolution and the Spartacus movement in Germany." The Hadji here mentioned the impact on his fellow intellectuals of *Revolutionary Culture, Revolutionary Mass Actions* and other books smuggled into the country. "I cannot overestimate the importance of this—the power of the printed word to influence book-hungry people who are struggling for knowledge and release. The Revolution and its literature also influenced many Dutchmen in Holland. As Communists and Spartacists were uncovered in Amsterdam and the Hague, the Dutch government hit on an idea to get rid of them. At home, they decided, such revolutionaries were dangerous; but in Indonesia they could do no harm. Here, dissidents would become privileged people, lording it over natives. They would love their sense of power and lose their sense of grievance. As Dutchmen, and white men, good jobs were arranged for them—teachers and principals of schools, officials in the civil service, high posts in banks and businesses, in railroads and telegraphs. It was a clever idea, but it backfired. These

124

Dutch Communists, converted into 'Big White Masters,' remained Red inside and acted under the discipline of Moscow. I wonder whether you realize now why we long ago lost respect for white, Western prescience. In dumping their Communists on us, the Royal Dutch Government helped to seal, not only its own doom, but Western imperialism throughout all of Asia.

"Soon many young Indonesians, Sukarno among them, became infected with communism. They infiltrated our nationalist movement. In 1922, when Senator McCarthy was still a boy, I was already exposing and purging Reds. We rid our ranks of them, only to be overcome by the Dutch Political Intelligence, which, as the Red threat grew more menacing, became more and more strict. In 1922, the party system was inaugurated. The Volksraad for a while gave our political parties some opportunity and scope. But the Dutch kept us weak by exiling any leader who stepped beyond the narrow limits of freedom the Dutch permitted. So you see, we were gaining experience with communism and fascism when America was busy with bootlegging and Al Capone.

"The Japs completed the split between the Dutch and ourselves. We offered to fight the Japs if self-rule were granted. The Dutch refused, and we opened our arms to the liberator. Every Indonesian remembered Djojobojo's prophecy—that the white people would be overrun by a yellow people from the north, but that in the time of one corn harvest, which means one generation, they would leave and we would be free. This legend was believed by all of us."

The Hadji rose, walked to his bookcase and took down several books—the Bible, the Ramayana, the Mahabharata, and a text on nuclear physics. "We believe in legends," he said, placing the books on the table before us. "We believe in much more than the eye can see or the mind can fathom. We believe there is as much truth in the Bible, the Ramayana and the Mahabharata as in this scientific textbook. It is not a truth that can be discovered in test tubes and retorts. It is a truth that exists in human experience. We do not accept materialism in any form, whether capitalist or communist. When I told this one day to an American journalist, he made believe he was going to be sick. 'Please, Hadji,' he said, 'don't you too give me Mr. Nehru's spiritual line. We are living, you know, in the twentieth century!'

"Christians generally accept ideas like the virgin birth and the resurrection of Christ—on Sundays. The rest of the time they are 'realists.' Well, we are not a Christian people. To us, the invisible world is as real as the world we can see. Something we Indonesians cannot understand is how Americans have the audacity to warn us of Communist atheism and materialism, when men like that journalist almost vomited in my face when I spoke of spiritual power.

"Neither are we happy to hear Christian overtones creep into your politics and diplomacy. You know, Christians say the Messiah has *already* come. The Jews say he *will* come. We Moslems believe the Messiah has not come and will not come until victory is achieved over all unbelievers. No idea that conflicts with Islam can win over our people. That goes for Christianity as well as communism. Therefore it is a mistake for America to introduce Christianity into its anti-Communist fight. Rather, you should study and understand other religions. Islam accepts the fact that all religions have the same origin but have been spoiled by conflicting revelations and interpretations. Mohammed said: 'I bring you no new religion. It is the same religion of Moses and Jesus. But get rid of those who came after.' All religious people share a great bond. It is severed only when one religion sets its conception of God and the spirit above all others. There is a lesson in that for America.

"Just as we do not take kindly to your sense of superiority in religious matters, neither do we take kindly to your advice and embargoes vis-à-vis the Chinese. China is remote from America, but we have been dealing with the Chinese for centuries as neighbors. We owe our soybeans and gamelan to China; Chinese money is still used in Bali. Our economy and culture are closely tied to theirs. We also know their bad habits —their greed and their cunning. We have had to cope with them all our lives. We think we know how to control them. Our laws are made not by Chinese, but by Indonesians. If you think we are soft on Chinese, look at how we are trying to build up an Indonesian bourgeoisie by discrimination against Chinese traders and industrialists. We supervise their schools, and we do not tolerate dual nationality.

"But our opposition to Chinese economic and legal imperialism does not cause us to sever relations with them. We live with them, we have intercourse with them, we do not cut ourselves off from them as America does and would have us do."

It seemed wiser to let the Hadji's thoughts and words flow without the distraction of argument. "As if that were not mistake enough," he continued, "America offered us guns to defend ourselves from Communist aggression. As a result, a Cabinet fell, and a legal door was opened for Communists to enter our government. A little wisdom, a little knowledge of the people you are dealing with, could have prevented that. However, the fall of a government need not be fatal. An election here can set matters straight. What it cannot put straight is the fact that America should have been willing to give us guns at all. Did you know to whom you were giving them? Did you know which way the guns might point? Did you expect that, having given us guns, you also could have pointed out the targets?

"To understand the folly of such an action, one must look closely at the Indonesian character. Originally we were animists, and to a degree we still are. Then came Hinduism. It taught us to renounce the world, to seek Nirvana. The Hindu influence remains strong. Then came Islam, which preached acceptance of life, acceptance of what God had given us, acceptance of our fate, and acceptance of personal responsibility. Then along came the West, preaching resistance, struggle, conquest. The Portuguese, the British, the Dutch—they wanted power and fought for it. We learned from them and won our independence.

"Today, we Indonesians are a mixture of all these philosophies—animism, renunciation, acceptance, resistance. We are struggling to reconcile these conflicting qualities within ourselves. We are trying to embody them all in an Indonesian philosophy. We are still in the process of searching for our souls. Not yet knowing ourselves, we hesitate to ally ourselves with one strong power or another. When others are so sure, and we are still groping, such an alliance would be fatal to our desire to find out who we are and to be ourselves. This is the root of our noninvolvement policy, and the root goes deep."

The Hadji's strength was ebbing, but sufficient remained for a final thrust. "Allies are notoriously untrustworthy unless they choose sides and fight with conviction. That America would arm us, a people whom she understands so little, is proof she will arm anyone. That does not speak well for her sincerity and good sense."

I thanked the Hadji but said I did not agree with some of his views, especially with his confidence that past experience with China was adequate to cope with its present-day Communist-sparked, Soviet-strengthened dynamism.

"I do not expect a son to agree with his father's words," the old man said. "I can only hope he understands that they are uttered with honesty, love and good intention. Perhaps, when you search for the reasons why America is so unloved and un-revered, it may help to give thought to these things. If nothing else, you may learn to see things from the point of view of an-other people. If you can learn that, America may discover some-thing no great power in history has ever learned—to identify its own cause with the cause of others, and to further that cause, not solely in terms of its own experience, tradition and desires, but of the experience, traditions and desires of others."

TWELVE

Pak Karto's Village

D AY AFTER DAY, Samiek, Bambang and I drove out to the rice and tobacco country surrounding Solo, observing, questioning, taking pictures and notes of every visible aspect and action of the farmers' lives. Often we were invited to have a meal, but from the bustle over the fires and the pretentiousness of the food I knew this was neither their daily fare nor their normal behavior. On one such occasion, I rose to relieve myself. Dismay shadowed the face of my host. Apologetically he led me to the kitchen. A large earthenware tub sat on the ground, into which water trickled through a bamboo pipe from some outside source. Food and utensils lay on the dirt, amid the excrement of chickens. With his eyes he gestured that anywhere would be all right. I escaped to a nearby field. When I returned, the man's pride was gone, and with it his hospitality. He murmured his humiliation at having so little to provide in comfort. His manner turned cool and we left as soon as we could.

Even after I became known in the villages, nightfall usually brought an end to my welcome. Every house was filled with its quota of humans and animals. The half-hoped-for, half-dreaded invitation to stay, to share their evening's leisure, to spend the

130

night on their earthen floor, to rise with them and live a day as one of them was withheld. It was not for lack of warmth or friendship, but for shame. Of all the barriers between Asians and Americans, shame born of poverty was the hardest to bridge.

Then, one evening, as we were racing homeward from a distant village to escape the storm that enshrouded Merapi and streaked across the plain, our car broke down. The full force of the monsoon struck us while we tinkered hopelessly with the engine. We pushed the car off the road and sloshed off in search of shelter. An ornate bamboo gate beside the road, topped with the words AUGUST 17, INDEPENDENCE DAY, advertised a village. A hundred yards down a lane we spied a cluster of houses and knocked on the door of the nearest. A man peered at us through a crack. Beneath the damp cotton batik covering his head and shoulders shone two bright eyes and a smile. He invited us in.

By the feeble light of a lamp I made out the figures of seven others huddling over a fire—a young, pretty wife, five children ranging from an infant to a twelve-year-old, and a grandmother whose teary eyes did not leave the simmering rice pot to greet us. Chickens and a goat grunted miserably in a corner, and doves burbled from rafters overhead. The room was dappled with their dried droppings. A mat was rolled out to form an island on the wet dirt floor. We sat down and Samiek explained about our mishap. The husband and wife exchanged a covert glance, and the man said we were welcome to stay. He introduced himself as *Pak* Kartodiharjo, a farmer.

While he, Samiek and Bambang probed each other's background for mutual kinsmen and friends, I took a second look at the room. It measured about fifteen feet by ten. Rain drove in through the split-bamboo walls, spattered through the tile roof, and seeped in from the ground. Pictures of Arjuna, Bima and Betty Grable wilted against a wall. The furniture consisted of two boxes, one for cooking pots, glasses and a mortar to grind corn, the other for a basket of rice and a block of salt. A large crock by the earthenware brazier contained water. The place was as damp and cold as only tropical houses can be when the sunshine fails. Although the children were wrapped in all the sarongs they owned, goosepimples roughened their bare legs and arms. *Mbah* (Grandmother) coughed harshly and salted the rice with her tears. Spooning the white heap, she said it was ready. Karto handed each of us a fistful of the rice, garnished with a bit of beancake and a wilted wafer of shrimp paste. We were eating silently when the door opened and two men entered.

One, a spare, serious-looking man, was the headman of the village. The other was a youngster dressed in a soldier's khaki shirt, trousers and cartridge belt, from which hung a pistol. After firing a barrage of questions at Samiek, the headman consented to our spending the night with Karto. He invited us to visit him next day before we left.

After the two had gone, Karto astonished me by saying, "You see, we too have an FBI." I asked how he happened to know about the FBI. He said that at the last wajang performed in the village, the *dalang* had made jokes about it. The FBI also figured in many American movies he had seen. He added that the people, once cut off from the world, now felt in touch with all that went on everywhere. His eldest son attended school and came home with all sorts of stories about America, Russia and China. Karto and his wife were also learning to write and read. Four hours a week a teacher taught classes in a Course for Common Knowledge on the headman's porch. Karto displayed his notebook. The last lesson consisted of a drawing of Bima's son, followed by a series of words utilizing the letters and sounds that formed his name, Gatutkatja. It ended with three sentences:

Our country is busy.
Chinese people become businessmen.
It is our own fault that we cannot save money.

Mbah said, "Even I can read a few words. Someday we will be clever enough to own our country."

"But you already own it," I said.

Mbah shook her head. "We own the air," she said. "The *belandas* and Chinese own everything else."

Karto said that every thirty-five days a team from the Ministry of Information came to lecture in the village. The last topic —Dutch refusal to give up Irian—had made a deep impression on *Mbah*.

Darkness and cold discouraged further talk. The family huddled on one of the mats; Samiek, Bambang and I shared another. The chickens, goat and doves ceased their restless stirring. Lulled by the rain drumming on the roof, I was almost asleep when worms in the bamboo mat found me. From the steady breathing of the others I judged I was the only victim. How, I wondered, writhing and scratching, could bamboo worms distinguish between *belanda* blood and theirs?

It was still dark next morning when the family awakened. The rain had stopped. The women and children disappeared outside to void and to wash. Then *Mbah* poked the embers of the night's fire, blew them into flame, and heated water for tea. We followed Karto to a stream near the house. Swollen by the storm, it rushed wildly through its banks, tearing at the walls of the bathhouse to which Karto led us. Karto rubbed his

133

hands and face with gravel and water, and rubbed his teeth and gums with a stick of charcoal. Then he squatted by the water's edge, defecated, and, lapping up water with his left hand, cleansed himself.

Dawn broke, suddenly and shining clear, while we were at our toilet. Walking back to the house, I saw, within arm's reach and growing wild, coconuts, bananas, coffee, ginger, oranges, mangosteens, rambutan and mangoes. Only the bananas were ripe, and Karto picked off a hand which made our breakfast. I asked *Bu* Karto, the wife, how much of her food she bought and how much came gratis from the fields and forest. She split open an orange and extracted the pits. Grouping nine pits in one pile and three in another, she said the larger pile came from Allah, the smaller from the Chinese grocer.

Bu Karto complained about high prices—three cents for a pound of salt, ten cents for a quart of oil, twenty cents for a yard of low-grade cotton cloth. It was months since meat had gone into her pot, at thirty cents for a pound of goat flesh. No one in her family had ever worn shoes. Only officials and Chinese could afford three dollars for such a luxury. To Karto and his family, luxury meant an occasional pack of *kretek* cigarettes, a caramel for the children, a visit to the movies. There was almost always a movie in the neighborhood, at *pasar malam* or evening fairs. For ten cents, the whole family could enjoy an American cowboy picture.

Karto rose and said he and his wife must leave for work. I asked if I might join them. We walked through the village to a neighbor's barn, where a buffalo rested on straw. Spying me, it rose to its feet, rolling its eyes and snorting fiercely. Karto asked me to hide while he soothed the animal. "Forgive him," he said. "He is not used to the smell of *belandas.*"

On the way to the fields encircling the village, Karto said he

134

had once owned a buffalo but it had died. With it had perished his future. A carabao was worth fifty dollars. He despaired of ever saving enough money to buy another. He owned only the ground on which his house stood, and his tools—a wooden plow worth ten dollars new, a harrow worth five dollars, and a *patchul,* a combined pick and shovel, worth about a dollar. His total assets came to forty-seven dollars. His debt to an Arabian moneylender was almost one hundred dollars. By Western reckoning, Karto and almost everyone else in the village were bankrupt. He sighed and said simply that life was hard. "Is it hard too," he asked, "for farmers in America?"

I said no farmer's life was easy, even though we substituted coal and oil for human energy. "Perhaps," I added, testing Karto's ability to understand me, "someday atomic power will ease the burden of farmers everywhere."

Karto smiled. "Tuan," he said, "in our village, all we hope for is a buffalo, one for each farmer. We do not ask for expensive engines, but iron rims for our cartwheels. We would be happier with things we can use today than with promises for tomorrow. The *dalang,*" he added after a moment's hesitation, "told us the difference between Americans and Communists. Americans talk about atomic power tomorrow. Communists talk about cheaper kerosene today."

Karto's task was to plow a neighbor's field, while his wife, working behind him, planted rice seedlings. For the three hours, from seven until ten, she would earn three cents, plus a half-pound of rice. He would earn seventeen cents for his labor, in addition to a small rice bounty. I watched while he harnessed the plow to the animal. It was a simple rig—a long wooden pole, a yoke on one end, a stick on the other. The lower end of the stick dug into the mud, the upper end served as a lever, on which Karto leaned when he wanted deeper purchase.

Karto guided the buffalo up and down the field by a line attached to its nose and flicked the beast occasionally with a whip. Sweat coursed down his body, irrigating the mud encrusting his face and chest. Itching to grip the plow and feel the buffalo's tug, I volunteered to spell him. He looked dubiously at the animal and at me, but he agreed.

I stripped to my shorts and waded into the warm, slippery muck. Karto handed me the rope and the whip. I flicked the animal's hide. Instantly the buffalo half leaped into the air and tore across the field. I leaned back on the stick and dug my heels into the ooze, to no avail. The buffalo vaulted the embankment and crashed into the next field. I skidded behind, gripping the plow, pitting my 150 pounds against the half-ton of furious, frightened bone and muscle at the other end. The buffalo tangled for a moment with the next embankment, giving Karto a chance to catch up, grasp the buffalo's nose ring and bring him to a stop. The beast glowered at me, heaving and stamping his hoofs. Wiping slime and sweat from my eyes, I backed away.

Karto calmed the animal and tied him to a tree while, with *patchuls,* we repaired the torn dikes. "It is better, tuan," he said, "if you drive your engines and leave our buffalo to us." I could not tell whether he spoke in jest or anger. Samiek was almost hysterical with laughter. Bambang said he had photographed the incident, but he wasn't sure his lens had stopped the action.

At ten o'clock we returned to Karto's house. *Bu* Karto weeded the corn, cassavas and sweet potatoes in the garden, while Karto cut wood and turned the tobacco drying on racks in the sunshine. The older children whittled *sate* sticks to sell in the market. At eleven *Mbah* produced a smoking batch of sweet potatoes and a pot of sugared tea. I ate greedily and tried to stifle the aching emptiness within me with a cigarette. The others seemed content with the meal, the elders smoking, the children sucking sugar cane. *Bu* Karto went to the stream to launder the sarongs soiled in yesterday's rain. *Mbah* ground corn and coconut for a neighbor's wedding feast scheduled for the following morning. Karto and the rest of us slept for an hour in the shadow of the house.

When I awakened, the policeman was waiting to escort me to the headman. His house, considerably larger than Karto's, had a stone *pendopo* or porch on which he and a stranger dressed in Western clothes awaited us. The stranger handed me a card engraved with the improbable name of S. Reboisier Soewarna—S, he explained, because it sounded distinguished. Reboisier, a French word he had found in a book, and Soewarna, "most charming." He was a police inspector, summoned by the *lurah* from Regency headquarters, about twenty miles away. My respect for the indigenous communications and security systems mounted.

Soewarna embarked on a polite but thorough inquisition into my identity and business. Neither my passport nor my explanation deflected his suspicion that I was a Dutch, British or American agent. His interrogation focused, more and more, on my motive in plowing the field that morning. Why had Bambang taken pictures of the occurrence? Was it perhaps to hold up his countrymen's primitive methods to American ridicule? Or did I plan to make propaganda, proving to the world how Americans worked shoulder to shoulder with his people in the mud of the paddy field? What, finally, was in my notebook?

I handed Soewarna the notebook and camera. "Take them," I said. "Read the notes and develop the pictures. I will wait here until you return them." Soewarna smiled, and the headman and Karto sighed with relief. Aside from my confidence that

137

the notebook and camera would sustain my innocence, I wanted an extra day to attend the morrow's wedding celebration.

The headman, treating me more like a guest than a hostage, led us on a tour of the village. His own house doubled as the *balai desa,* or town hall. The porch was used for meetings, elections, banking and other civic business. His living room differed from Karto's chiefly in its furnishings—a table, several chairs, and a battery-run radio, the only one in the village. A newspaper lay on the table. The *lurah* generously permitted me to borrow it. The house faced a square or common, bordered by a mosque for men, another for women, a religious school for children, the people's school, and the clubrooms of the local chapter of the Muhammadiyah or Moslem society. In the center was a pool stocked with carp. None of the buildings was architecturally pretentious, the mosques, schools and residences all being simple oblong boxes of split bamboo. Beyond the common, under a holy tree, sprawled the market place, on which, every Wednesday, farmers and merchants from miles around converged. It was empty today. Near it stood the office of the government salt monopoly.

A bulletin board outside the town hall displayed Ministry of Information posters, the current edition dealing with the impending elections. Hammer-and-sickle emblems, captioned "Communist and Non-Party Candidates," adorned trees and walls. One house bore a twin sign: "Communist Party Headquarters" and "Farmers' Union." The headman said that the Masjumi and Nationalist parties maintained offices in a nearby town.

The afternoon suddenly turned taupe. Rain pelted down, driving us back to the headman's house, where we spent the rest of the day discussing the village's affairs. The headman explained that the only officials in Indonesia elected by democratic

138

process were headmen. All officials above him were appointees of Djakarta, a situation which the impending elections would, of course, change. His own assumption of office had occurred four years before, upon the death of the former *lurah*. Every man and woman in the village over eighteen had gathered outside the town hall. Friends had nominated several candidates, each identified by a symbol—a banana, a goat, a buffalo, a fish. Boxes, similarly marked, had been set on a table. Each voter had dropped a stick in the box of his choice. By count of the village elders, the present headman had won. He would serve until incapacitated by illness or death, or until disqualified by poor performance of his duties.

These were many. He officiated at every birth, wedding, death and divorce. He served as adviser to the village co-operative and bank. Once a week he reported personally to the assistant head of the prefecture; once a month he met with the wedana, the prefectural chief. Every visitor who arrived in the village, every sale of land and cattle, every celebration and disturbance was known, within a week, by the *Residen,* or chief of the province. Most onerous of his duties, said the headman, was tax collection. Families with incomes under $180 a year could plead inability to pay taxes and win a hearing. Practically every family claimed such exemption, and it was his difficult task to grant or deny their pleas. Four families in five won their appeals; only 56 out of the village's 242 families had paid taxes for the current year. He showed me the tax audit. Eight families with incomes between $350 and $400 had each paid thirty-five cents in taxes. Twenty-two families with incomes between $400 and $500 had each paid up to seventy-five cents. Twenty-six families with incomes between $500 and $1,000 had paid from one to three dollars in taxes. Larger incomes, up to $1,200, had been taxed up to five dollars. There were nine such families,

four of them Chinese merchants and millers, the others Javanese farmers.

The village derived additional income from a salary tax of 3
per cent levied on earnings for work performed for others, and
from rental fees charged for market-place stalls. Total revenues
came to $412.32. About half was paid over to the treasuries of
the county, province and national government. The remainder
was the village's to spend as it wished. Twice a year all heads
of families attended meetings to decide, by vote, how funds
should be expended. Road repairs, irrigation and officials' sal-
aries—including those of the headman, the teachers, and the
policemen—usually consumed every cent.

The headman received about three dollars a month as salary,
but he had the right to farm and crop one hectare of communal
land. For each birth, marriage, death, and each sale of cattle he
recorded, he received five cents. Each sale of land entitled him
to 5 per cent of the price for preparing the deed. As an executive of the village bank and co-operative, he earned about
twenty-five dollars. He also was paid a small stipend by the
provincial government. Altogether, in the last year, his income
had been about $180 plus the yield of his land.

Land, said the headman, was the village's only real wealth.
It was measured in *ubins,* one *ubin* being equal, according to my
crude computation, to three square yards. Three thousand *ubins*
comprised a hectare, about two and a half acres. One hundred
and seventy-two families owned less than a tenth of a hectare.
Fifty-two owned from a tenth to a half a hectare. Fifteen owned
from a half to one hectare. Three families owned from one to
four hectares. The *lurah* frowned. "Every year the amount of
land remains the same, but sons and daughters multiply. We
cannot stretch Allah's goodness much further. Someday we will
be too many. Then we shall starve."

140

I asked how the dilemma could be solved. "Transmigration," said the *lurah*. "At least half of the young people must go to Sumatra, Borneo or the other islands where land begs for people. Many want to go and have listed their names with the transmigration office. But money to transport them and get them started is lacking. Whoever would help us to conquer our jungles would truly be Indonesia's friend. There, not here, lies the future of our nation."

It seemed to me that young men like the *lurah,* having proved their popularity at the rice roots, and with obvious administrative ability, might someday be pushed by the people into positions of national importance. I asked him whether he had ever been encouraged to travel, study, develop his abilities. He said the Communists had offered to arrange an invitation to visit the Soviet Union. As a good Moslem, he had declined. He had never received such recognition from the United States, nor, to his knowledge, had any other *lurah.*

Back at Karto's, that evening, our meal consisted of rice and pepper, fried in coconut oil. My hunger was aggravated by the array of food prepared for the wedding and awaiting delivery to the neighbor's house. After eating, Karto hauled down a cage from its perch atop a tall pole by the door and drew out his finest pigeon. With a number of friends, each with his own bird, there began the customary evening sport. One man stood a distance away, ruffling a female in his hands. The others, at a signal, released their males. Karto's pigeon, named Cloud, was first to spy and swoop down on the female. Karto picked up his winnings, a cigarette, and we all adjourned to a neighbor's house to smoke and talk.

After exchanging a few lewd stories, the men discussed the impending marriage. It was time, they agreed, for the boy and girl to wed. He was seventeen and a radio technician in the

141

Army. The girl was a ripe fourteen. His parents had combed the villages for miles around for a family of equal rank with a marriageable daughter. They had settled on a girl in this very village and had sent a friend, known for his eloquence and guile, to sound out her parents. Veiling his mission in circumlocution, he had managed to weave in praise of the boy and his family. The girl's father had responded by hinting of his daughter's beauty and virtue. Later, the two families had met at the girl's home. At the proper moment, she had entered the room and served tea, giving the others their first chance to appraise her appearance and demeanor. After this ritual, known as *nontoni*, or "taking a look," the guests had left to think things over. As a soldier, the son had demanded some say in the final decision. In describing this, Karto and his friends admitted that times were changing, and that today's youth, exposed to school, movies and military service, no longer were sheep. Happily, the son had approved his parents' decision, and a letter was dispatched proposing marriage.

The girl's father, it seemed, had meanwhile undergone a change of mind. Unimpressed by the financial status of the boy's family, he had urged refusal on the grounds that the birthdays of the children augured an unhappy union, and also because an older daughter remained unmarried. The mother, unwilling to take the risk of having two spinsters on her hands, had overcome his objections, and a letter of consent had been dispatched. Both families then had met for a *ningseti* or bindfast ceremony, and had fixed a wedding day in obedience to the astronomical calculations of a *dukun*. A gold ring, a batik sarong and a bodice were given to the bride by the groom's parents. Tomorrow, at the altar, the couple would meet for the second time in their lives.

Next morning, at six-thirty, relatives, neighbors and friends, dressed in their best, arrived at the bridegroom's house in a nearby village. We passed under a bamboo gate bearing the greeting: "Welcome to all our guests." We men took seats on the gaily decorated porch; the women disappeared within the house. A light breakfast was served. The groom appeared, a rather glum-looking lad dressed in a black mess jacket and sarong. Shortly after, the guests, the older men first, formed a column behind the groom and walked to the home of the bride. To make certain that the spirit world was tranquil, special offerings of food and flowers had been placed at every crossroads along the line of march. Upon arrival, the groom, flanked by a family friend and the father of the bride, faced the headman in the center of the room. The *lurah* read the marriage certificate, pledging the groom to pay two dollars as a token purchase for the bride, and forbidding him to leave his wife except for good cause. The groom assented.

A screen was removed, revealing the traditional *ngalam* or altar of pillows, symbolizing nuptial bliss. It was decorated with banana and waringin leaves, the banana meaning hope for a large family, the waringin hope for peace. Before the altar sat the bride, a child of extraordinary beauty. The young hair around her brow was gathered in eleven clusters. Her costume, a black, gold-embroidered jacket and sarong, was aflame with flowers. Rising, she greeted the groom at the threshold, then stooped to wash his feet. The couple sat down together and fed each other with their fingers. The bride's father then held his daughter on one knee, the groom on the other, and asked his wife, "Which is heavier?" She answered, "Both are equal," expressive of their acceptance of the groom as their own son.

Bride and groom departed for the house of the groom's father. We followed and examined and approved the nuptial bed, banked with flowers, wajang puppets, and wedding gifts, including a large floral wreath garnished with red ribbons and the symbol of the Communist Party. A feast was served, with special food for the spirits of the dead, for the evil spirits of the world, for Adam and Eve, for unity between the in-laws, and for the good fortune and peace of the married couple. It was interrupted by an announcement of the couple's new name. Since the groom was a radio technician involved in the transmission of messages, the name chosen was Sastradihardja, "writer of many letters."

In neither village was any work done that day. It was a time of restrained joy and feasting, culminating at night in a wajang performance on the *lurah*'s porch. The *dalang* explained that usually, on a wedding night, wajang dwelt on stories of love-making and the conception of children, but that tonight another theme had been chosen. It was to honor a stranger, a *belanda* from America, a man who could tame atoms and all the thunder and lightning of the universe, but who could not control a carabao. The audience roared with laughter. The *dalang* then described the general situation in which the evening's play was set.

"We are in the public square of Madiun town. We see Musso, leader of the Communists, speaking to the people about independence. He tries to arouse the people. He says each man, to be truly free, must have his own hectares of fertile sawah. But Musso's words belie his true intention. Musso's secret desire is to become the strongest man in the land, more powerful than Bung Karno."

The gamelan played and the *dalang* waved into position the puppet-images of farmers, soldiers, politicians. His voice changed to match the character of each actor.

Musso: "My children, we are independent now. The government has not yet given you the rights you fought for!"

144

People: "You are right, *Pak!* We have not got what we shed our blood for!"

Musso: "Now we must unite and fight to throw out the government, for it has fallen into the hands of foreigners. We must end, once and for all, all vestiges of colonialism!"

The meeting ended and the puppets disappeared. The *dalang* continued: "In every kampong the Communists hold meetings. When the time is ripe, their soldiers seize and imprison government officials and all leaders of parties who will not co-operate with the Communist Party and the Pesindo. The struggle increases with killing, shooting, knifing and throat-cutting until the villages are red with blood!"

The puppets rattled and clashed with increasing fury. Suddenly President Sukarno and Vice-President Hatta appeared before the screen.

Sukarno: "Brothers and sisters, stand fast! Be loyal! We will put down this revolution in one month or less!"

The *dalang* staged another furious battle. "Soldiers of the government," he announced, "shoot down or capture the Communist Pesindo. Musso disguises himself as a cart driver and tries to escape. But a clever soldier stops him."

Soldier: "Who are you?"

Musso: "I am just an oxcart driver from this village."

Soldier: "Where are you going?"

Musso: "I am leaving because my village is a battlefield, and dangerous for a peaceful man like me."

Soldier: "Are you a member of a party?"

Musso: "No, I am just a peaceful villager."

The *dalang's* voice quavered with excitement. "But the soldier looks at Musso's hands. The hands are not those of a cart driver. They are the smooth hands of a Communist politician. Musso realizes he is trapped. He runs, but the soldier shoots

145

and Musso falls. The other Communists are caught and jailed. Bung Karno visits them in prison."

Sukarno: "Children, you have done wrong. You must go back to a good way of living and serve your country in the spirit of the Pantjasila."

Prisoners: "*Wah,* Bung Karno, you are right! Let us go home and we will never again be disloyal."

Hatta: "You have the right to join any political party you desire. But it is not allowed to destroy the government. Our President is Bung Karno. We must unite with him and defend our country."

The *dalang* concluded the evening with a final, solemn chant:

> *For a man to do his duty*
> *It is not so easy.*
> *He must not hold back.*
> *He must serve his leader forever.*
> *He must obey his orders.*
> *He must not be misled by evil doers.*

After the performance, I asked the *dalang* how he came by the information he dramatized so effectively for the villagers' edification and enjoyment. "I have eyes and ears," he said. "I listen to the winds. I read the newspapers. They give me many ideas."

"From tonight's wajang," I said, "I would judge you are an enemy of the Communists."

"I am nobody's enemy," the *dalang* said. "I am simply a teller of tales."

Next morning, S. Reboisier Soewarna returned with the notebook, camera and a packet of photographs. "We could not condemn you for what you have written," he said. "It contains no secrets about our country. But even if our suspicions had been confirmed, and you are a propagandist, the pictures make one thing certain. You are not a very good one."

Karto and his family said goodbye with a gift of a giant pineapple. The *lurah* headed the procession to our car and made a fine speech of farewell. As we sped toward Solo, I opened the packet of film Soewarna had developed and printed. Apparently the buffalo had been too fast for Bambang's hand and lens. With one exception—one showing the animal and me eying each other with mutual trepidation—every picture was a blur.

THIRTEEN

The Bull's Head
under the Press

ANY REMAINING ILLUSIONS that the people were oblivious to the crosscurrents that lapped their island home were dispelled by our visit to Karto's village. That their culture was saturated with political significance had come as no surprise. That schools and movies were smashing the walls of illiteracy and ignorance behind which, for centuries, the people had been imprisoned was further affirmed. Now, in addition, I had glimpsed the *dalang*'s power to mold popular opinion. And in the headman's house I had seen the two instruments through which news filtered to the *dalang,* the *lurah* and the people— the radio and the newspaper.

I gave the *lurah*'s newspaper to Samiek for translation, and set out for the market to buy a radio. A Chinese shop displayed a few American sets, tagged at more than two hundred dollars. From their age, I judged they were in small demand. More popular was a simpler model manufactured by Phillips, a Dutch company, in Surabaja. Nicknamed, because of its size and shape, Radio Roti, or bread-loaf radio, it cost thirty-five dollars. Even

148

at this price, radio ownership was limited to the wealthy and to officials, restaurant owners and innkeepers who used them to inform or attract the public. The clerk in the post office to whom I paid my twenty-five cents monthly radio tax said there were almost three thousand licensed plug-in sets in Solo, a city of three hundred thousand. In the villages, however, ownership of sets, all battery-powered, declined to about one per ten thousand families.

Broadcasting in Indonesia was a government monopoly. My set brought in three ten-kilowatt government stations in Solo, Djokjakarta and Semarang. The signal from Djakarta was too weak for easy listening. My efforts to bring in the Voice of America from San Francisco or the Philippines were futile, nor could I pick up any broadcasts from the Soviet Union or Peiping. Only a transmitter stationed in or near Indonesia, more powerful than the government's, could have covered the country. Consent for such an operation, officials assured me, was unthinkable.

Every morning, at six o'clock, broadcasting began with the announcement: "This is Radio Republic Indonesia Surakarta," followed by the strains of "Lovely Ambon," a popular tune. An hour of music ensued, mostly Indonesian, but with a gratifying number of Connie Boswell recordings. At seven, a half hour of news, national and local, was presented, in the main, objectively. After seven-thirty, the airwaves were silent. Then, at 1 P.M., came two hours of *gamelan* music, interspersed with one newscast. Silence again until, at five, the evening program began with a half hour of songs and stories for children. Five hours of Indonesian and American music were broken by four newscasts, an announcement of new laws and regulations, and a digest of editorials and articles from current newspapers and magazines. Fifteen minutes were allotted to complaints and com-

149

ments from listeners, mostly appeals for more wajang. Wajang performances, lasting for hours, were featured five times a month, not enough, apparently, to satiate the audience's appetite. At ten-fifteen, the station signed off with last-minute news relayed from Djakarta, and a final rendition of "Lovely Ambon."

Conceivably, the Nationalist Party in power could have used its control of radio to slant news programs even more than it was doing. It did not press its advantage in the programs we heard. Samiek said all parties vigilantly monitored the broadcasts; any dereliction would quickly result in complaints in Parliament and in the press. Eadie and I thought the programs pleasant, innocuous and, newswise, preoccupied with national and local affairs. Other countries seemed able to win radio time either by the engaging quality of their cultural output, or by actions that impinged on Indonesian interests.

The United States, with its song-hit recordings, did rather better than any other outsider on the cultural side. Politically, the Soviet Union and Communist China excelled. Communist dignitaries were frequently reported as visiting Indonesia and other Asian countries, always armed with a word or gift precisely right for the local mood or situation. We kept hearing about their presentations of books to Indonesian libraries and universities, and their concern for Indonesian health, prosperity and peace. The United States, by contrast, seemed almost always to be rattling its sword. While we were tuned in, Radio Indonesia never broadcast a single kindly American deed or word contrived at its source to win Indonesian applause. America's vaunted talent for creating a favorable press and radio reaction to a product or personality mysteriously deserted it at its borders. When the Soviet Union's promise to build a steel mill in India won a minute on Radio Indonesia, while America's millions in

Asian grants and loans earned nothing but silence, we wondered whether America's publicists and press agents had all defected.

The borrowed copy of the headman's newspaper, translated by Samiek, compounded our wonderment and concern. Entitled *People's Sovereignty*, half of its four pages dealt with local and national news, such as an order of its commander praising the loyalty of Indonesia's Army, plans for Djokjakarta's two-hundredth anniversay celebration, the sentencing of an official in the Ministry of Economics for embezzlement. Advertising consumed another fourth of the space, and international news the rest.

In this last category, page one featured a picture of the Ambassador of the People's Republic of China, on its fifth anniversary, shaking hands with the Prime Minister of Indonesia. Another story described the gift of two volumes on the life of Gandhi to Red China by India's Ambassador in Peiping. These items were balanced by two concerning the United States. One was heavily headlined: AMERICA TO REARM GERMANY. The other: MARILYN MONROE ASKS DIVORCE. Linked to the latter was a piece captioned: "Nurnaningsih, Indonesia's Marilyn Monroe, called by police for questioning on charge of posing for nude photos." A final international news note mentioned the Ottawa conference to discuss the Colombo Plan.

Page two's big overseas story told of Hasan Tiro, "ambassador" of the so-called Indonesian Islamic Republic, a dissident group, testifying before the Security Committee of the United States Senate about communism in Indonesia. A second piece dealt with the admission of Captain Franken, a Dutch agent, that he had supplied arms to Dar Ul Islam terrorists.

Page three's foreign news featured a photograph of America's atomic cannon, snapped at NATO maneuvers in West

Germany. A second story described a banquet given by Mao Tse-tung to foreign diplomats, at which he pledged China's devotion to peace. A third played up the strike of London's dock workers, which paralyzed Britain's biggest port. A fourth reviewed a new American motion picture, *Man Crazy*. "From the beginning to the end," it said, "you can see the bad character of each girl, and her bad way of living." Page four was taken up by advertisements for aphrodisiacs and patent medicines, plus the day's radio schedule.

Only *Suara Merdeka (Free Voice)*, with a daily circulation of 16,000 copies, reached a larger audience than *Sovereignty*. After reading these papers for several days, I concluded that both had been captured, if not by Communists, at least by the Left. To meet the men who published them, and to learn generally the mechanics of the fourth estate in Indonesia, Samiek and I again took to the road, heading for Djokjakarta, the home of *Sovereignty*, and for Semarang, the source of the *Free Voice*.

The editor of *People's Sovereignty* graciously received me in his modest home. I had half expected to meet a dour Communist. Instead, Wonohito proved to be an open-faced, jovial young man who talked enthusiastically about his recent visit to the United States, under the auspices of the American Press Institute.

"There were fourteen Asians in our group," he said. "We attended a seminar at Columbia University. In Washington we had a press conference with Ike and visited the Senate as Dick Nixon's guests. Then the group broke up. I went to Geneva, New York, and lived with the editor of the local paper, the *Daily Times*. After that we had a week in Decatur, Illinois, five days in the New Orleans YMCA, three days in Los Angeles and finally a week in San Francisco and Monterey. We had been warned about the color line, but we had trouble only once, in

New Orleans, where the white waitresses at a drugstore lunch counter wouldn't notice us. Even they eventually concluded we weren't Negroes and served us.

"We went to America with a prejudice against it. I'd been told America was materialistic. The Dutch had always said, 'America is big, but it has no culture.' I quickly learned the opposite is true. In Geneva, the family with which I lived actually prayed before dinner. I have seen many American moving pictures, but I never knew Americans said prayers. I never knew a stranger would pick me up in New York and spend hours showing me the city. That didn't fit the old saying that in America 'time is money.' I had a real problem adjusting to American women. The movies had given me the idea that American women go around half naked, looking for sex, and were punched and treated cheaply by American men. Instead I met the much-honored Mother of the Year. I could hardly believe Americans celebrated Mother's Day and treated their women with such respect.

"Most impressive, I think, was the willingness of Americans to be friendly with me, a colored man. One night in Decatur, Dr. Gage of the history department of Millikin University had me at his home for dinner. I met all his friends and answered all their questions about Indonesia. Next day he sent a letter to the Indonesian Ambassador in Washington." Wonohito showed me the letter, calling it one of his most prized possessions.

"My family and friends," Dr. Gage had written, "were delighted to have become acquainted with Mr. Wonohito, whose personality, character and knowledge were so noteworthy. You should know that he was a worthy representative of his people, leaving with us a lasting impression of excellence. We learned from him, and our affection for your new nation and its people is deepened."

153

"No one can convince me that people who will do a thing like that are materialistic," said Wonohito. "And Dr. Gage is not alone. Every month I receive letters from friends in America. 'Dear Won,' they write. Can you imagine that! To be given a nickname like that is what I like about America!"

"Feeling as you do about my country," I said, "why does the newspaper you edit take such an anti-American line?"

Puzzlement overspread Wonohito's features. "My newspaper is not anti-American," he said. "It simply presents the news. The bulk of the news we get from America deals with armaments, war, your anti-Communist phobia. When your Secretary of State handed a pistol to Mr. Naguib, or threatened massive retaliation, did the newspaper in Geneva, New York, suppress the news? It did not. Then why should I?"

"But Won," I said, "the United States is spending millions abroad for peaceful, constructive purposes. How can you be silent about that, and at the same time play up mere promises of Soviet aid?"

"Surely," the editor replied, "you know the American definition, 'When man bites dog it's news.' It is hardly news when another shipload of American fertilizer arrives in Djakarta. But when Russians offer aid, that's news. When your fertilizer arrives, I receive a trite paragraph from your official propaganda agency. When Russia opens a crack in its pocketbook, every commercial wire service in the world magnifies it into a cornucopia. Americans, who can dramatize sex, crime and war so well, always manage to smother the drama in their foreign aid. You can hardly expect me to handle your activities more imaginatively than you do yourselves."

Wonohito lit a cigarette and leaned back in his chair. "Please try to understand me. I admire America. It is big, rich and strong, and determined to do the right thing in Asia. But it is

154

so ignorant of Asia and Asian people. When I said I came from Indonesia, many people shook their heads. 'What a pity,' they said, 'that Ho Chi Min is turning it into a Communist country! What will happen,' they asked, 'after the French are kicked out?' Or, 'Where is Indonesia?' they'd ask. 'Is it near Siam?' Everyone in America knows Siam, but very few seemed ever to have heard of Indonesia. When people are so ignorant, you wonder how sincere they are about their interest in Asia.

"Also, the minute you meet an American, he asks about communism. 'Is your country Communist?' 'How strong is your Communist Party?' 'Why isn't your country on our side?' When I talked about noninvolvement, they shook their heads. 'Wake up, Won,' they'd say. 'You've got to be for us or against us. In this day and age, every nation must stand up and be counted!'

"Nowhere, in all the countries we visited on our trip, did we find such egocentric people as the Americans. They know they are right, that their way is best, and that settles everything. Nevertheless, when America says the gracious thing about my country, when it acts with understanding of my people, when it breaks through the ice of diplomacy and does the little things that reveal warmth, appreciation, true friendship, believe me, it will be on page one of my newspaper."

On the road to Semarang I pondered the cruel paradox. The more generous America's actions, the less newsworthy they became, and the more sensational, by contrast, Russia's cynical promises. The wound was not assuaged by the thought that year after year, American industry managed to present its products with imagination, novelty, surprise. Why, then, did American aid descend to the trite? For all the injustice in Wonohito's argument, there was enough logic in it to make me burn.

The editor and publisher of *Free Voice* offered no comfort. A burly man who affected an American sport shirt and slacks,

Hetami salted his English with slang, and minced no words in answering my questions. He too had been invited by the Institute to visit the United States, but he had declined.

"What good would be accomplished to go from here, where I am needed, to America, where I am not needed? I want to raise my self-respect, not have it lowered. I want to be a better Indonesian, not a better American. But," he added, "don't get me wrong. I don't hate America. Neither do I follow her. You still think force, speed and high pressure are the way to solve problems. You are still obsessed with your frontier psychology. You see danger everywhere, you shoot from the hip. America can never win Asia that way.

"Sometimes I think you are jinxed. You manufacture atom bombs. You want to test them. Where are they dropped? Always in Asia and never near places where white men live. It creates a bad impression.

"You proclaim yourselves as democratic. To prove it, Americans have asked me to arrange an interview with our Regen, and then they arrive in blue jeans.

"You are wounding us grievously with your moving pictures and automobiles. A country like Indonesia needs constructive movies, not sex. We need little cars, not expensive show-off cars. We need useful books, at prices we can afford, and what arrives from America? Soft drinks!"

Rather than listen to a repetition of the Coca-Cola argument, I asked Hetami to explain how his newspaper was started, where it got its news, and how, generally, it was managed.

"As a country becomes more literate," he explained, "newspapers become more important. That is why, in 1950, my wife and I started this newspaper. Most other newspapers belong to rich men and political parties. We felt the field was open for a nonpartisan paper, formed a holding company with money borrowed from family and friends, and began to publish *Suara Merdeka*. In 1953, with twelve thousand circulation, we started to break even. Today, at sixteen thousand, we're making money. Our chief competition is *Sinmin*, Chinese and Red, with eight thousand readers, *People's Sovereignty* and *National*, each with ten thousand and middle-of-the-road. Total newspaper circulation among Central Java's seventeen million people is sixty thousand copies. But these people are all influential—officials, students, teachers, others who trust a free newspaper more than the government's radio or other official sources of news. They spread the news to their servants and others, and pretty soon whatever we print is picked up by the *dalangs*, bus drivers, and peddlers and is talked about in the kampongs.

"Our chief source of news is Antara, a foundation controlled by its shareholders who also are its subscribers. Antara takes the services of America's United Press, Britain's Reuters, France's AFP, Red China's Sin Hua, Yugoslavia's Tanjing, Russia's Tass and the Dutch ANP. It edits them and sends us flimsies. We pay three hundred dollars a month for Antara's domestic and foreign service. We also pay one hundred dollars a month to Press Bureau Indonesia for domestic and foreign news, and thirty-seven dollars a month to an American concern, King Features, for mats, features and Roy Rogers."

Recalling others' reports that Antara was government-subsidized and that it had a clear pro-communist bias, I asked Hetami how the editorial policy of his newspaper was determined.

"I set it myself," he said. "The only pressure of which I am aware might be called national sentiment. Even the Party-line papers, whose policies are set by political overlords, must heed it. Many, I am sure, have grave doubts about our claim to Irian and believe we ought to put our own house in order before we look for trouble abroad. But they daren't put that in their pa-

157

pers. It would be opposing the 'national will,' and that can be financially and physically dangerous. The Ministry of Information controls the paper supply. They could find reasons for cutting it off and putting a newspaper out of business."

Hetami took me on a tour of his plant. I congratulated him on its cleanliness and efficiency. He was pleased and led me to the modern press. "See," he said, "it is made in America. So are the linotype machines. The whole plant is organized and run in an American way—as freely, I think, as any respectable American journal. But here, buried in the floor, beneath the press, is the head of a bull, to protect us from evil spirits. Think over the meaning of this. When you understand it, you will understand Indonesia."

FOURTEEN

The Doctors
and the *Dukun*

SEVERAL MONTHS after our arrival in Indonesia, sickness struck us. The children were feverish, Eadie was out of sorts, and I was wracked by constant headaches. For Jill's and Arthur's sake, we debated the advisability of returning home at once for proper care. Eadie's decision was to stay. "We came here to learn all we could about these people. Well, let's see what happens when someone gets sick."

It was good that we stayed. Otherwise we might not have met Naioka, the *dukun*. She resembled a mummy—seventy pounds of skeleton tautly covered with amber skin. White hair, drawn back from the forehead and knotted at the neck, accentuated the smooth roundness of her skull. Her eyes were shadows, and inside her toothless mouth the cheeks must have touched. Somehow, her macabre features added up to an air of wisdom, dignity and grace, and her smile was sweet. No one knew her age —we guessed not a year less than eighty—but as a healer her reputation was second to none.

During our first months in the community, we had paid her

scant attention. To us, she symbolized Indonesia's animist past. Although superstition and sorcery were deeply rooted in local custom, they were doomed, we thought, in the modern state to which the people aspired, and we gave our time to the study of less exotic matters. But Naioka, without our suspecting it, had her cavernous eyes on us. The first intimation of her interest occurred in a food stall near her house, where, one day, I was eating *sate*. Completely addicted to these delicious morsels, I rarely passed the little place near Naioka's without stopping for a snack. This day she padded across the road to talk to me in a dialect I could not understand. Other customers sitting around the charcoal brazier did, and, when they had controlled their laughter, they explained. "Naioka says you like *sate* very much. If you keep eating it, she says your wife will have another son."

Eadie enjoyed my report of the incident. A few days later, however, she was wincing with pain. Years before, in a skiing accident, she had wrenched her back, and now she felt the first pangs of the since-recurrent trouble. Doctors at home had never succeeded in diagnosing or treating the symptoms. Over the next few days it became clear that this was to be no ordinary seizure. She lost weight and, as though to favor the affected region in the lower back, assumed a hunched, twisted posture, which our neighbors noted. They urged us to call in Naioka.

Although we had formed a deep respect for the wisdom and ways of the kampong people, we were not quite ready for a witch. We turned, instead, to Dr. Heintz. He palpated Eadie's back and had X-rays taken at the hospital. Like so many American doctors before him, he guessed that the pain was caused by a slipped vertebral disc pressing on a nerve. Treatment called for special equipment which stretched and snapped the spine throughout its entire length, until the vertebrae fell into place. Indonesia boasted no such equipment, and he could do nothing except advise rest and provide a few pills from his meager stock to ease the pain.

Far from easing, the pain increased and Dr. Heintz conferred with his superior, Dr. Suwito. A handsome Javanese of middle age, trained in the Netherlands, Dr. Suwito headed the orthopedic department of the local hospital. In addition to being one of his country's most eminent physicians, he was a talented *srimpi* dancer and wajang performer, in the finest classical manner, and headed Indonesia's Cultural Congress. Surgeon, public servant, administrator and artist, Suwito's typified the careers of the pitifully few trained Indonesians whose young nation needed, and cast them, in many diverse roles. With Dr. Suwito, as with Dr. Heintz, we formed close personal ties which helped mitigate the disappointment of their negative findings.

It was at a conference to discuss these findings that Dr. Suwito echoed our neighbors' suggestion—to summon Naioka. Dr. Heintz hardly bothered to mask his horror. To Eadie and me, it seemed a rather poor joke. But Dr. Suwito was serious. "Her knowledge is different from ours, but not, for that reason, valueless. She has effected many cures for which I, a doctor, cannot account. At any rate, Western science has failed, so why not try the East's? In calling Naioka, what have you to lose?"

The question pricked the bubble of pretense surrounding our mission. We had come to seek knowledge of an Asian people. We had found them culturally advanced, politically sophisticated, intellectually subtle. They commanded our respect. We deeply believed that if a harmonious relationship between Asians and Americans were ever to come about, it must rest on mutual respect, on our willingness to take as well as to give. Now, at the first test—the test of personal acceptance of an Asian value—we flinched. Deep down we felt that we did indeed have something to lose—not life, not health, but something, rather, that I called self-respect and Eadie labeled our sense of superiority.

"Let's face it," she said. "The very idea of an American woman being treated by a witch doctor sounds worse than ridiculous. It strikes us as degrading, demeaning, a step down the ladder of civilization."

Eadie sent Sindo to Naioka's house. He returned and said we should expect her the following morning.

Naioka arrived about ten o'clock and stood quietly at the door, staring at Eadie. Through Sindo, who spoke her dialect, she gave her orders. She wanted Eadie to lie down on her bed, and she sent Sindo for a cup of coconut oil and a plate of limes. When these arrived, she climbed astride Eadie's hips and began to probe the entire surface of her body with long brown fingers. Her hands were finely boned, the veins and tendons as distinct, beneath the mottled skin, as in an anatomical drawing. They paused at the abdomen and at the small of the back as though they had discovered the trouble's source. Then, dipping her finger tips in the oil, she whispered a few words as in prayer, moved to the bottom of the bed, and began to massage the soles and toes of Eadie's feet. Her fingers burrowed into the flesh, reaching for muscles, tendons, nerves whose existence, Eadie later reported, she had never suspected. As the fingers inched up, almost imperceptibly, the apprehension in Eadie's eyes vanished, the lids closed, and she submitted, relaxed, as though in sleep.

Two hours later the massage ended at Eadie's scalp. The patient slept. Sweat glistened on Naioka's forehead, but otherwise the tiny old woman showed no sign of the ordeal. She walked to the veranda, squatted on the floor, and asked Sindo for tea. Our children watched in awe while she drank, and her eyes rested briefly on them. Then she set down her cup and murmured something to Sindo.

"Tell the tuan to rub the madame for a few minutes every hour, everywhere but the stomach. After three days, she will stand up straight. Tell him that within the year he will have another son. And tell him that he, his wife and the two children all have malaria."

She rose, and, giving me time neither to question her, nor to thank her, nor to pay her, she left.

Three days later, Eadie felt fine. Not long after, she knew she was pregnant. And Dr. Suwito's blood tests showed we all had malaria. Our reaction to all these developments was, mildly stated, mixed. We were as delighted at the news of a new baby as at Eadie's recovery. We were worried about the malaria, although, at the moment, the only symptom was a persistent moistness of the skin which we had been blaming on the climate. And we were puzzled by Naioka. How had she made such accurate diagnoses? How had she succeeded, where so many doctors had failed, in curing Eadie's back? How could so frail a woman possess such endurance and manual power? Was there something Asia's witches knew that Western science had missed? If *dukuns* could cure illnesses that baffled physicians— and Dr. Suwito assured us that our experience was far from unique—was Western science as necessary, as benevolent, as effective in Asia as we Westerners had been led to think?

"Only Naioka can explain her method," said Dr. Suwito. "I cannot. All I know is that the answers to your questions do not lie entirely in the field of medicine. The total philosophy and outlook of our people are involved. A Western doctor looks at a heart and sees an efficient pump. An Asian sees also a capacity for anger, sadness, love. In Holland they taught me to test the human ear with certain sounds. When I said there

163

are sounds the ear cannot hear, sounds audible only to the spirit, they called me a superstitious fool and almost threw me out. Western medicine is limited largely to the physical; its tendency is toward more and more specialization in the body's separate parts. In the East, we are concerned with the entire human potential, spiritual as well as physical. Naioka would not recognize bacteria if she saw them, but she sees something else. I don't know what it is, but I do not scoff at it just because I do not understand it."

Dr. Heintz laughed. He had recently twisted his ankle, and he pointed a cane at the damaged foot. "I spent five years studying that ankle," he said. "I know its every bone, cartilage, artery, vein and nerve. I have a lamp to bake it and the newest analgesics to reduce swelling and pain. Would you recommend, doctor, that I throw all this out the window and call your witch?"

Dr. Suwito shrugged. "No. But as a mortal I am conscious of my fallibility. As a doctor, I am aware of the limitations of physical science. As an Asian, I believe there is more to life, to the human body, to disease than meets the microscope's eye."

"All right then, doctor," said Dr. Heintz facetiously, "I shall pack up my microscopes and return to Leipzig."

Dr. Suwito smiled, but a touch of grimness edged his reply. "Please, Heintz, do not bait me. You know how badly Western science is needed here. We can use all we can get. We regret only that, while we accept your science, you laugh at ours. This is bad, medically, because since the West cannot claim complete knowledge, it should not balk at unfamiliar thresholds. It is also bad in other ways. Nothing disturbs an Asian so much as your failure to concede that we, too, may have a little to contribute."

Heintz, the doctor, remained unpersuaded. But on Heintz,

164

the refugee, Suwito had scored a hit. The German stared at his bandaged foot. "Well," he said, "this does not cure the malaria. We have a little Aralen. The children should start taking it at once. Perhaps you can buy more on the black market. If not, there's the native quinine."

Dr. Suwito added, "And Eadie had better start her prenatal right away. There's a gynecologist at the hospital I'd like her to see."

The hospital was a vast complex of one-story buildings and courtyards, built by a Dutch religious order fifty years before, and taken over, after the revolution, by the government. Altogether, there were four institutions of its type to serve the three and a half million people in the province. Their thirteen doctors and eleven hundred beds were in heavy demand. We felt badly about adding to the burden, but Eadie's obstetrician, a beautiful woman named Dr. Sumi, would listen to no apologies. "If it weren't for your Rockefeller Foundation, I would not be a doctor. It gives me pleasure to repay a debt."

A woman with a medical degree was rare in Indonesia. We were frankly curious about how Dr. Sumi had overcome the handicaps of poverty and custom. She explained that it had been largely a matter of luck. "My father happened to be a civil servant, a modern man, who made great sacrifices to educate his children. And Indonesia is not so backward that a bright girl cannot get ahead. The real obstacle was the hard work, the strange language, the lack of books and equipment in school. Until I entered the University of Indonesia, I had never held a test tube. Even today, our high schools have no laboratories or equipment to prepare students for the sciences. In medical school, many of the courses were in English. But we had few American books and practically no English-Indonesian dictionaries. Luckily, the Rockefeller Foundation had trained many of

165

our teachers, who helped us overcome our lack of knowledge and equipment by writing out passages from the textbooks in Malay. Today, English is our second national language, and the American Information Service is supplying books. But students face difficulties almost as great as my own. Of those who enter the medical schools, fewer than 10 per cent win their degrees. At that rate, it will take a century before we have enough doctors."

Nor did matters end there, according to Dr. Sumi. "Vivisection is contrary to Moslem law. Autopsies can be performed only by special court order. Many of us never saw the inside of a body—human or animal—until our first operation. It is quite a jump from models and charts to living tissue. Whatever competence we eventually achieve we owe to our patients. Their outlook on illness and pain is shaped by the wajang. It teaches them to take an impersonal view of life, to act and to suffer with detachment. Dutch women I have delivered scream with pain and demand anesthetics. Our own people suffer silently."

Dr. Sumi's voice dropped to a whisper. "I remember one amputation I did during the war, with nothing but a tourniquet to numb the leg. The man had lost two sons in the fighting. I told him how sorry I felt. He smiled. 'I am happy, doctor,' he said. 'My wife gave birth to another son in the midst of the battle. Just as the baby was born, a mortar shell exploded. Weren't we lucky? No rajah ever had a better salute!' "

In an average month, Dr. Sumi and her colleagues treated 12,575 patients, mostly for malaria, ulcers, syphilis and beriberi. Every day, she performed eight major and fourteen minor operations, in addition to deliveries. She remained on duty twenty-four hours a day. The hospital supplied a bed and meals. Her pay was $79.25 a month.

Eadie occupied, for a while, a private room in the hospital.

166

For a dollar a day she had her own bathroom, clean linen, good food, and a nurse whose services she shared with four Chinese patients. Dr. Sumi frowned when we expressed our pleasure. "To you, a dollar a day is little. But for most Indonesians, it is a fortune. A few can afford second class, with eight patients in a room, or third class, with twenty-two. But most can pay nothing. They are sent to the fourth class. Would you like to see it?"

Fourth class proved to be a vast barrack with 180 beds—noisy, dirty and jammed with sick of both sexes and all ages, and with their families, who provided food and other services the hospital could not furnish. Dr. Sumi gestured helplessly. "These people have heard of modern medicine's miracles. They want its benefits. This is what they get. Back in the kampong and villages where they come from, there are no surgeons, no iron lungs, no antibiotics. But neither, where life and death are concerned, is there class distinction. Whatever the *dukun* has to give is shared by rich and poor. To many of these people it seems that in Western medicine the determining factors between life and death are position, privilege, money. Many leave here cured in body, but scarred in spirit."

On an evening when Drs. Suwito, Heintz and Sumi all happened to be visiting, we mentioned our dismay that the most humanitarian of Western efforts should, in curing physical wounds, create social and political tensions. Dr. Suwito remarked that it was inevitable. "Everything new imported into a poor country—whether it is Coca-Cola, Cadillacs or penicillin—creates new desires that didn't exist before. As long as the supply is limited and the price high, the result is social tension. In a country with less than one doctor for every sixty thousand people, no wonder there is anger when they see rich Chinese in private rooms, or in the doctors' offices, while they queue up in an outpatient clinic. The trouble is that it may take fifty years, at the present rate of progress, for medicine to catch up. Meanwhile, dissatisfaction festers. The next ten years may decide Indonesia's future."

"What's the answer?" Eadie asked.

Dr. Suwito broke the ensuing silence. "Naioka," he said. "Every village in Indonesia has someone like her. The *dukun* is the people's midwife, nurse, druggist and doctor. For a thousand years, she has been our medical practitioner. She has been respected, feared and loved. To undermine confidence in her is to knock out one more prop under our village social structure. Loss of face turns her into an enemy. Destroying her invites a long period of doubt and disquiet about public health. I would rather have Naioka as a friend. It is better to strengthen her than to destroy her. It seems wiser to add to Naioka's knowledge, and to build upon it, than to compete with it or replace it. I think, if we did, Naioka could not only save more life but also ease us through the hard days ahead."

Dr. Sumi nodded, but Dr. Heintz wouldn't budge. "A capital theory," he said, tapping his cane on the floor to emphasize his words, "but it disregards two factors. The West will subsidize medical students, but not witches. And you can't get a witch to go to school."

Whether Dr. Heintz was right about the impossibility of getting Western support for an indigenous medical-improvement program, we had no way of knowing. But we could, and did, find out how Naioka felt about the idea. She fixed herself a cud of betel nut and lime, and mouthed it for several minutes while thinking over Dr. Suwito's words.

"Long ago," she said finally, "a *belanda* boy—a white man's son—was bitten by a snake. The Dutch doctor said he would die, and his mother brought him to me. With Allah's help, I saved his life. When the mother went again to childbed, she called me to help her instead of the doctor, and she died of fever. The doctor called me vile names and threatened to beat me. But from his anger I learned that, had my hands been clean, the woman would have lived. Ever since, I have washed my hands. If what the doctor taught me in anger could be given with love, it would be good. I am too old to learn new ways, but my daughters would walk to Semarang or Cheribon if someone were there to teach them."

Then Naioka added, "Tell the madame that a woman with child must have mountain air and the food of her own people. Give her no quinine or she will abort. Tell her to take her children and go away."

Eadie thanked her and asked how she could repay her. "A *dukun*," said Naioka, "is merely a messenger of Allah, and Allah asks no fees. One pays what one can. It is always enough."

With the help of our neighbors, a fee was finally agreed on, admittedly high, but one that, it was felt, we could well afford. It was eight rupiahs—about forty cents.

Months later, after our return to New Hampshire, Eadie had a fine son. And we received a letter from Dr. Suwito. Among other items was this: "Dr. Heintz's foot was no sooner out of bandages than he slipped and twisted it again. *'Liebe Gott,'* he shouted, 'get Naioka!' "

FIFTEEN

"Sumatra—or Bust!"

AFTER NAIOKA'S WARNING, Eadie and I took stock of our situation. We agreed there was little point in lingering in Solo. Familiarity was already blurring the first, fresh image. While each day revealed some hitherto hidden facet, repetition was more the rule. I decided to check our material on Central Java by a quick swing around the rest of the island. Eadie and the children, meanwhile, would undergo treatment, rest, and ready themselves for the homeward trip upon my return.

Every part of Java I visited was unique. Each deserved the same intensive study we had given Solo. In Surabaja, for example, I attended a performance of its famed *Marhaen Ludruk,* or People's Theater. Burlesque in the Minsky manner, it featured female impersonators, lewd skits and, in addition, hilarious political satire, of which the Dutch and the rich were the chief butts. East Java's theater lacked the wajang's beauty and polish but, like Central Java's richer cultural forms, provided a forum for political propagandists and a valve for releasing popular tension. So effective had it been during the Japanese occupation that its best-beloved clown, for mocking the Emperor, had been stood against a wall and shot.

Similarly, the dance and music of the Sundanese around Ban-

170

dung differed in expression from the Javanese but throbbed with the same cultural pride and political significance. Sporadic terrorism in the countryside prevented visits to the villages, but even from my train window the poverty of the rural areas around Djakarta, and in vast areas of the west, contrasted cruelly with the lushness of the central plains. These provinces, too, were cursed with a variety of landlordism.

I returned to Solo with three convictions. The first was that centuries of suppression had imbued the mass of Javanese with political acumen and subtlety. The second was that it was impossible to overestimate their cultural and national consciousness and pride, or their hunger for education and fullest freedom, or their will to strengthen their own indigenous mechanisms of government and finance, or the impact of the collision between their traditional way of life and the West's, especially America's. The third was that Java was groaning under the weight of its human burden, and that its resources, however rich and highly developed by modern techniques, must, in the end, fail to feed the mouths of coming generations.

It was with special interest, therefore, that I read the message awaiting me from the headman of Karto's village. Remembering my interest in resettlement, he invited me to attend a meeting to recruit migrants and to bid farewell to a group whose applications for land in Sumatra had been granted, and who would soon be on their way. It was an invitation I could not resist.

Only the posters on the bulletin board and walls had changed since my previous visit. One contrasted starving slave laborers under the Dutch and Japanese, leveling forests under the guns of grim guards, and happy farmers clearing land today. The caption read: "Transmigration, then and now." A second poster pictured a happy family on its way to new lands and opportuni-

171

ties. "I had no land," it was captioned, "and so I am migrating."

The meeting, held on the porch of the headman's house, was attended by about a hundred young men and women. The *lurah* introduced an official from the District Transmigration Department. Like so many of Indonesia's civil servants, he was young and eloquent.

"The government," he said, "realizes that for many of you food is short, and some of us even go hungry. That is not right when we are rebuilding our country. Our meeting is held to discuss this matter and to find a solution.

"The reason is that there is not enough land here in Java for all of us. As each new child grows up, he too wants land. Each year the people increase, but the land remains the same. Yet thousands of hectares in the other islands call for arms and backs to clear and plant them. In such places there is plenty of land for all. To move from here to there is the best answer to the problem.

"Sumatra is three and a half times bigger than Java, but it has less than a third as many people. In Java, four hundred and fifty people are crowded into every square kilometer. In Sumatra, only twenty-eight people occupy the same space. In Kalimantan, only five people, in the Moluccas and West New Guinea only two people live in each square kilometer. Here, land is scarce. There, it is going to waste.

"If you decide to move, the government will pay your family's fare, give you land without cost, and lend you seed and tools. Until your first crop is harvested, it will also give you food. Think this over carefully. All who want to go need only to leave their names with the *lurah*."

Farmers asked, "How much land will we get?"

"Two hectares," the official answered.

"What kind of tools?"

"A *patchul*, a sickle, an ax."

"How much do we get until our first crop?"

"Starting the first day you leave, you get five cents a day, and free transportation from here to your new home. You are loaned tools, building materials, food and clothes until the crop is in. After six months, you must repay what you borrow."

"What happens to us if we cannot pay our debt?"

"Our experience is that everybody can pay it back in two years. You will not be punished if you take a little longer."

"What happens if I don't like it?"

"You may return any time you want, but you must pay your own transportation and repay what you have borrowed from the government."

"Can we live there as we do here? Is there gamelan music and wajang?"

"At first you will be too busy clearing the jungle and planting. Later, you can live as you please."

The meeting over, the people scattered to their houses to discuss the proposal. The official smiled. "It is always the same. The women are fearful. Most men, too, look at their beloved village and fields and decide it is better to be satisfied with what they have than to risk life in a hostile jungle where tigers lurk behind every tree. But some will take the chance."

His prediction proved right. Next morning, eleven families volunteered for Sumatra. Their names were entered on a list. The *lurah* advised each to live normally until, perhaps many months later, they were notified to get ready.

Nine families, after a year's delay, had just received their notice. The week had been spent in farewell parties. Subdued and apprehensive, they carried their babies and bundles down the lane to the highway where a bus waited. In Solo, at the

173

Transmigration Office, a doctor examined and certified them as fit for the journey. The group settled down in a nearby kampong and ate a meal of vegetables and rice. About a hundred migrants from other villages were already in occupancy. The men squatted in tight circles and exchanged what little information they had about the new country.

Early next morning the contingent boarded the train for Merak, the embarkation point in West Java. The trip took the better part of a day. The travelers hung from the windows, gaping at the unfamiliar scenery and gasping at the unsuspected size of their island. Officials met us at the station and marched the group to a barracks near the docks. At the sight and smell of the sea, some women and children wept. The men tried to comfort them, but their faces, travel-worn and worried, betrayed their own mounting doubts about the wisdom of what they were doing. Tears and doubts dried, however, when each family was issued thirty yards of cotton cloth, a pan, a pot, a dried fish, salt, twenty pounds of rice and two bottles of coconut oil. No one could remember ever having had such a bonanza, and the barracks rang with laughter and song.

At five o'clock the following evening we boarded the *Merak*, a steamer of uncertain age and tonnage. My cabin had a clean berth, running water, a toilet and a steward who brought me a delicious *nassi goreng*, fried rice and egg, each time I rang a bell. The migrants blanketed the open decks, fore and aft, resting their children amid their heaped-up possessions and eating cold boiled rice. The farewell blast panicked the youngsters, who were not reassured by the terror in their parents' eyes as the land receded. The Sunda Strait was ripped by turbulent tides, and the ship's heaving induced an epidemic of nausea. The decks were soon awash with spew. Throughout the night, families wept, prayed and clung to one another for comfort.

174

Spirits rose as dawn exposed the palm-fringed golden beach and green mountains of Sumatra. The *Merak* docked at Tandjung Kareng, where officials checked off the passengers against lists and led them to a cluster of buildings a half mile from the beach. Large, well-built structures, picturesquely located under towering palms, each consisted of a long corridor flanked by platforms, on which the families were invited to make themselves at home. An official announced that food was ready in a nearby kitchen and pointed to a row of toilets, a bathhouse and a laundry area a short distance away.

The men brought rice and fish from the kitchen to their wives and children huddled on the platforms. Though the terror of the sea voyage was over, the impulse of all but a few was to cling together, to talk, sleep, comb their hair or inventory their belongings. "None of us," a young farmer shyly admitted to me, "has ever been away from his birthplace. None of us has ever before been to sea. We do nothing but worry. Only because there are so many of us do we have the courage to go on. But many of us already regret our decision."

I joined one of the officials at a refreshment stall on the beach. He waved his beer bottle at the barracks and shook his head. "If they are frightened now, what will they do tomorrow night, in the jungle? If they knew the truth, they would go back on the *Merak*."

A child died that night and was buried before daybreak. Burdened with gloom, the others boarded buses and headed inland. All morning, progress was swift, over a smooth highway lined with villages and neat farmland. After a stop at noon for food and water, patches of forest thickened into an unbroken wall, tangling overhead and darkening the sky. The pavement vanished. The bus lurched over a rocky trail ending, in late afternoon, in a clearing. The driver said it was Suka-

175

radja, our destination. Into a single bleak building trooped the bedraggled pioneers. Night fell before the last family was settled on the platform. A few unwrapped remnants of rice saved from lunch and ate. Others sat in the semidarkness, numb with fatigue and terror, listening to the noises from the encircling wilderness. I lay on the floor and shut my eyes. I had read about America's pioneers, of their loneliness amid danger, but until now, I realized, I had never really fathomed their ordeal or their courage.

Dawn did little to relieve the general misery. The children were first to venture outside, but, fearful of the forest, they clung to the house like vines. The women rocked and moaned on their platform perch, and the men gathered in groups to curse themselves for their folly. In midmorning, an official arrived and said they would remain in Sukaradja, chopping trees, expanding the clearing and improving the road. When this was done, the land would be divided into two-hectare plots and each plot numbered. Each head of family would draw a number from a box and would be given the plot marked with its number. He could then choose between taking possession of a ready-made house, built by government contractors, or, in lieu of a house, seventy-five dollars.

A farmer asked the official which, in his opinion, was better. The official shrugged. "Good carpenters might be wise to take the money. But most of you are farmers. It might be better to take the house and start work at once on your crops."

The prospect of work, of land, of homes excited everybody, and a buzz of talk cut through the gloom. The official suggested that I go along with him to a rendezvous with a Ministry of Information man who was visiting all the villages in the area to talk about the general election. "Nothing will happen here for months except felling trees and burning brush. I suggest you travel with the information man to some of the established villages. You will see what Sukaradja will look like in a month, six months, a year."

Hope was born in Sukaradja that afternoon. Armed with axes, *patchuls,* honing stones and long knives called *goloks,* the men attacked the jungle. The ring of metal against wood, the crashing of trees sent spirits soaring. As we left, children were playing tag among the stumps, and the men were singing.

The information official, when we met, was delighted to have me join him. A gaunt youngster in his early twenties, named Amat, he drove his jeep expertly over the almost invisible trail that threaded through cracks in the jungle wall. Tightly woven vines cast darkness everywhere, and, though the skies were sunny, occasionally we needed our headlights. I was harried by dysentery and Amat made many stops. Each time I floundered a few feet from the jeep, tripping and falling among the roots. Once I could not retrace the few steps to the car, and I shouted to Amat to blow his horn. The screeching of monkeys, birds and insects answered. Then I heard Amat cough a few feet away. Sweating with weakness and fear, I climbed into my seat and we drove on.

Trees sprawling on the ground, mountains of them, gray, dead and marked with axes, announced a village. Beyond stretched semicleared fields, corn and dry rice growing amid the charred rubble. The trail became a muddy street, lined with about forty houses. Amat said it was Punggur, settled a year earlier. The houses were all alike, fifteen feet by twenty-one, with wooden walls and thatched roofs. They stood on stilts to discourage snakes and other animals, and each had a small porch beneath which goats and chickens scrabbled. It was just before dark, and women chatted on the porches, children played

177

on the road, and men worked among the rotting stumps, cutting, weeding and burning.

We spent the night in the house of the headman. After a meal of rice and pineapple, the most delicious I had ever eaten, the *lurah* lit the cigarette I gave him and reminisced.

"In Java I was a coolie in a batik factory, earning two dollars a week. It was enough until I married. After the children came, and my parents and sister moved in with me, we often went hungry. When I saw rich men and Chinese with plenty of food and fine clothes, I almost went crazy listening to my children cry for rice. When the Transmigration official came to our kampong, he made me think. Maybe life would be better in a new place, where I'd have a piece of land. I talked it over with my wife, and in January I registered my name with the Transmigration office.

"They told me I could choose Kalimantan, Sulawesi or Sumatra. I remembered that someone in the kampong had gone to Sumatra and had written good things about it, so I chose Sumatra. We arrived here eleven months and nine days ago and went to work at once, burning the brush and hauling away the trees. We left the stumps just as you see them. In another two years, they will rot away. We were given fifty pounds of paddy seed, five pieces of corn, ten pounds of vegetable seed and seed for ten fruit trees. We planted the seed between the stumps. We quickly learned that our two hectares were really worth only one, because half the land could not be cleared. Each month, until the first harvest, we were issued twenty pounds of rice per person, two dried fish, four pounds of salt, and a half-liter of oil. To earn enough for cigarettes and things we needed for the house, I cut wood and sold it to the tile factory in the next village. Now we are getting along by ourselves."

I asked the *lurah* whether his family was happy.

"My wife and children still cry at night, especially since the death of our third child. There was no *dukun* here to help, and the spirits were unfriendly. Anyway, the baby lies in unholy ground and my wife worries about the strange spirits who live near its grave. Also, there is no school for the older child, and no gamelan, no wajang, nothing to do in the evening. As for me, with so much work, I have no time for worry or tears. I am happy except for two things. I have never received a paper to prove this land and house are really mine. The officials tell me it is all written down in the book at Metro, but how do I know they tell me the truth? How can I be sure that after I have cleared the land, someone might not come along and drive me away?

"Our other worry is the soil. The older farmers with experience say it is good for three years. After that, irrigation will be needed. The officials tell us not to worry, that the Department of Public Works will build irrigation. But they do not carry out their promises. All the money goes to Java."

A few miles down the road from Punggur lay Purbolinggo, a venerable community settled in 1952. Here, though stumps and charred trees still defied man and nature to dislodge them, the houses had paint, fences and flower gardens, and at the cross-roads stood a school and several shops. Our host, Samadi, a thirty-year-old Javanese, was one of the original settlers.

"In West Java," he said, "land is owned by the rich and sold only at high prices. Most of us worked for the landowners, on their promise to pay us half the crop. But before the harvest, we had to borrow rice to live on. When the crop came in, the landowners took it all in payment for the debt, and we were left with nothing. Some of the younger men formed gangs, and they robbed and killed until no one felt safe. Here we have tigers, but I fear a tiger less than a landlord or a desperate man with a gun.

"The government paid each of us twenty-five dollars for clearing the land. We farmers held a meeting and decided to form a co-operative. Each paid in five dollars. Formerly we had always paid *idjon,* borrowing two pounds of paddy from a Chinese miller and paying back four. Now the co-operative bought many tons of paddy at thirty dollars a ton. After the first harvest, the government bought one hundred tons at forty-two dollars a ton—a profit of twelve hundred dollars.

"Bad weather spoiled our seed that year. Again the co-operative saved us. Each member borrowed seed on the promise to repay the original amount plus an extra amount to be placed to his credit in the village godown. I borrowed two hundred pounds and put back two hundred and fifty. We saved paddy until, in two years, we have a profit of over three thousand dollars. We are going to buy a bus with it. With a bus to take us to Metro, we won't feel so far from the rest of the world. And we can ship our rice and vegetables to the market.

"Already the co-operative has driven the Chinese out of business. It sells oil, sugar and cloth cheaper than they could. At our last meeting, someone proposed that the co-operative go into contracting. Instead of having outsiders come in to build houses for new settlers, why shouldn't we sell our wood and labor and take the profit ourselves? In ten years I hope to tear down this house and build a new one, big enough for my family to live in comfort, with a tile roof that doesn't leak. For the first time in my life, I can make plans like that. Even for talking like this, people would have laughed at me in West Java.

"Our only worry is the land. It was not good in West Java either. But here it leaches out even faster. We need water. We need fertilizer. The officials tell us engineers are coming to

180

build canals. They had better hurry. Our crops this year will be less than last."

For a week, Amat and I coursed the jungle trails from village to village. After a while I could guess almost to a month when the community had been settled. The newer ones were primitive and bleak but eager to apply the paint, plant the flower gardens, build the schools, mosques, markets and even moving-picture theaters that gave their older neighbors substance and comfort. Except in veterans' communities, where the Army supplied a few tractors and trucks, the wilderness was being razed by hand tools and sweat.

In each village, Amat spoke to assemblies about the impending elections. "When you build a house," he said, "it must be strong so that hard winds will not blow it down. When you build a nation, it must also be solid. In Indonesia, the government's strength is the will of the people, expressed in its Constitution, its Parliament and its laws. When you vote, therefore, for the men who will write our Constitution and laws, your heart must be clean and your eye watchful." Amat then described the election process, warned against fraudulent registration and violence, and invited questions.

At similar meetings I had attended in Java, questions had been many, and reflective of deep economic and political malaise. Here the people seemed anxious to end the discussion and get back to work. Mainly, they wanted assurance that Sumatra's interests would not be overlooked in what they believed would be a Javanese-dominated Parliament. "For the first time in my life," one citizen said, "I have work and land. I ask nothing from the government but water. Without water, we will die. Will the new Parliament forget the promises made to us, or will it remember?" Amat admitted Sumatra was outnumbered

181

by Java. "All the more reason," he said, "to elect representatives clever and strong enough to demand your rights."

I remained as far in the background as possible at these meetings, lest I be accused of meddling in Indonesia's election. At one session, however, a villager rose, pointed at me, and asked if I would tell why America's elections were so beset with bloodshed and crime. Amat insisted that I answer. I said our elections were peaceful, in the main, and characterized by national acceptance of the majority's will. Where, I asked, had he got an opposite impression? From the ensuing hubbub, I gathered that an American moving picture, unnamed but resembling *All the King's Men*, the superbly moving drama of Louisiana's fight against political corruption, had deeply impressed the villagers, more with its violence, clearly, than with its impeccable moral. I decided that the situation warranted a defense of America and of the freedom of its arts to criticize every aspect of our national life, including elections. Sensing that I was coming perilously close to a speech, I ended my remarks abruptly with the word to which all Indonesians respond with enthusiasm— Freedom! To my chagrin, the audience laughed.

En route to the next village, I asked Amat the reason. At first he refused to tell. At my urging, he finally answered. "Your speech was very good until the end, when you meant to say *merdeka,* freedom! Instead, you said *mantega,* butter! But do not worry. The people understood."

Though I never again broke my rule against mixing in Indonesian elections, I was interested in Amat's speculation about the results. "The Javanese," he said, "are crowded together. With so many people, and so little land, their situation is hopeless and they know it. The youth, especially, with all its education, has doubts about finding work. So in Java, people rub together and become tinder for the Communist match. Here,

182

however, people are scattered and busy, with little time to listen to Communists. That is the importance of transmigration. When people can spread out and breathe, they don't fall for Communist lies. The pity is that what should be a deluge is just a trickle. Neither our politicians nor yours appreciate and help the movement of people to the land. The result may be that the oil workers in Palembang will push the island leftward."

Our tour ended in Metro, a jewel of a city, incongruously set in virgin jungle. The mayor, who spoke an almost colloquial English, proudly showed off its handsome schools, mosque, Catholic church, and its paved streets and neat bungalows lit by electricity. I could hardly credit his account of the city's development. Started in 1935, its growth was interrupted by the Japanese and was not resumed until 1952 by the Republic. Now 108,000 people lived in the Metro area on 18,000 farms, totaling 750,000 square kilometers of cleared land. Each of its farms averaged four tons of dry paddy a year. In 1953, they produced thirty thousand tons worth over a million dollars, of which half was exported.

The mayor admitted the land needed irrigation and fertilizer. "Nevertheless," he insisted, "this land is rich. We produce tapioca, we process our rice, we export lumber. We are rich in all but one thing—people. In 1954, fewer than twenty-one thousand people came here from Java. That isn't many. In fact, only five hundred thousand people have migrated to Sumatra since 1905. The island is still empty. It can easily absorb sixty million people. Numbers are not important, but people are. Here life is hard. But we have no usurers yet, and no *rumah gadais*. If a farmer needs money, he goes to his *lurah* and asks for a loan. He can borrow four hundred rupiahs at four-per-cent interest per annum. Or he can join a co-operative. Here co-operation is essential, because no man can defeat the

183

jungle alone. Sumatra breeds co-operatives. And the co-operatives breed thrift—and capital. Capital enough to finance the next season's crop and start a small charcoal or pottery industry. The old habit of wasting resources is broken. A new way—of sacrificing a little, saving a little—is transforming not only the land, but more important, the people."

The mayor talked as indefatigably as he walked. He paused at last before a movie theater. The current feature was an American Western, *High Noon*. The mayor gestured toward the blood-stirring posters.

"Our youth walks miles to see movies of America's Wild West. They crave romance, adventure, wealth. Yet here is the real thing at their very door. Our nation has a slogan, 'Out of many, one.' We should add another—'Sumatra or Bust!' "

An American shared my compartment on the train from Metro to Palembang. He introduced himself as an agricultural technician with the United States Foreign Operations Administration. An elderly man with an air of wisdom, he listened to my impressions of the resettlement area and shook his head.

"History," he said, "is filled with grand schemes to move people from one place to another. Usually, they were tragic failures."

"Sometimes," I said, "they are brilliant successes. For example, the United States."

The technician frowned. "Sumatran land deteriorates rapidly under cultivation. Farmers encounter problems in land management they never ran into in Java, and worse than anything we know in the States. The soil leaches so rapidly, nourishment drops below the plant roots. Yields fade from forty to twenty to ten kilos of rice in three years. One answer is laydown farming.

Clear, cultivate, harvest an area, then leave it for five or ten years and go elsewhere. You can't do that with manual labor. Here bulldozers are needed to clear the forest, tractors are needed to plow in green manure. You have to figure on scientific management—rotation, equipment, fertilization and all the rest. In short, it is a problem of land development. The Indonesians have the wrong slant on it. They see it purely in terms of people."

I said I wasn't sure I understood the difference.

"Well," he said, "the right way to look at Sumatra is through a microscope. What is important is the chemical content of its soil and water. The wrong way is to see Sumatra in terms of people. Once you do, you are dealing, not with scientific truth, but with human emotions."

I asked whether it wasn't possible to combine the two.

"Nonsense," he said. "The two don't mix."

SIXTEEN

"Independence
Is Not Enough!"

PALEMBANG, straddling the river Musi on the northern fringe of Sumatra's resettlement area, staggered me. Few man-made structures equal in complexity an oil refinery. Here, rising sheer from the wilderness, were two, Stanvac's and Shell's. Tankers suckled at the discharging end of pipelines that stretched, behind a maze of smokestacks, storage tanks and giant retorts, to the oil fields, hundreds of miles distant. Here, in a single frame, were Asia in the raw and the near-ultimate in industrial technology. No American could view it without a thrill of pride in what it represented—the vision, courage and efficiency of foreign enterprise at its biggest and best.

What did it mean, though, to the twelve thousand workers who, mornings, crossed the river to the smoking steel behemoth on the other bank, and who, evenings, returned from the twentieth century to their bamboo shacks? To them, was it exploitation, or development, of their nation's resources? Were their white managers hated intruders, or welcome teachers and friends? What human emotions were being generated within this tangle of boilers and pipes? Were they, like the oil and gas Palembang produced, controlled and propulsive, or explosive and wild? These men in white helmets and dungarees, armed with Stillson wrenches and acetylene torches, looked a different breed from Java's farmers and Punggur's pioneers. I decided to learn what they were like.

As a start, I put my questions to the director of Palembang's Ministry of Labor. "My task," said this youthful but tired-looking man, "is to settle disputes between the companies and the unions. I must be, and am, impartial. But truth compels me to say that the companies' policies are the most advanced and enlightened in Indonesia. No Indonesian firm treats labor so well. Even I, a high-school graduate and government official, am less well paid and receive fewer benefits. Yet the workers are not content. To find out why, I suggest you talk to their union leaders."

The secretary of the Indonesian Islamic Labor Union spoke quietly, with great conviction. "Our union," he said, "has one goal: a society in which everyone enjoys prosperity by carrying out the orders of Almighty God. Those orders are all written in the Koran. Takatsuk, the chapter on wealth, says: 'To accumulate wealth is a sin. Accumulation is the wrong way to heaven.' We are against class struggle. Baqoroh says: 'There is only one struggle and that is against tyranny and cruelty.' We believe in unity of the workers. Ali Imron says: 'Unite within the religion of Allah and be not divided.' We want a free, sovereign Indonesia, dominated neither by America nor by Russia. Ameigah says: 'Only he without sin shall inherit the earth.' Only he is without sin who acts in accordance with the Koran. To follow the lead of others is to take the path to Hell.

"And so, for a Moslem worker who seeks to better his wages and conditions of labor, there is but one way: to heed the words

187

of the Prophet. The Communists believe Marx, and Marx says there is no God. No Moslem, therefore, can be a Communist. Communists are loyal to Russia. No Indonesian can therefore be a Communist, for an Indonesian worker must be loyal to Indonesia. Communists believe in class struggle. Islam believes in co-operation between owners and workers.

"But neither," the secretary continued, "can a Moslem worker be a capitalist and loyal to America. In America, life is divided into separate compartments. Culture is one thing, politics another, economics a third. Every few years, you follow another leader or idea or theory. But Islam teaches that life is one— there is but one Book, one Prophet, one Church, one God. In capitalistic America, you are rich one year and poor the next. First, inflation. Next, a crash. Each man tries to get along as best he can, stepping on his neighbor's body to save his own. The strongest, the cleverest, the best-educated rise while men less fortunate go down.

"Islam is against all that. We believe that society is more important than the individual. We want educated people to use their intellects *for* the less-well-educated, and not *against* them. We believe the owner of a business has a social function in the life of the worker. He must act for the prosperity of the worker. If an owner has a car, so must the laborer have a car. As the owner eats, so must the worker eat. That was Mohammed's way until Islam was defeated. Now that Indonesia is free, we must restore Mohammed's way in our daily life."

I asked whether he had ever discussed labor's role in the United States with an American labor unionist. "Never," he said. Nor had he or his union received any publications dealing with America's economy, and the changes that, with organized labor's help, had overtaken it in the past fifty years. "All I know about America is what the moving pictures show and the

188

newspapers print. It is always strikes, violence, crime and racketeering."

How, I asked, did Islamic concepts affect his union's relationships with Stanvac and Shell? "At the moment," he said, "not at all. We have never called a strike against the companies. That is not our purpose. Our purpose is to build an Islamic Indonesia. Once we succeed, Stanvac and Shell will conform to Moslem law."

Practically all labor trouble in the oil fields, refineries and rubber estates were instigated by Perbum, the Communist union. To my surprise its leader consented to meet me in the labor official's office. In his early thirties, thin, bespectacled, tense, Simandjuntak spoke English rapidly, punctuating every few sentences with my name.

"Our union," he said at once, "is strong for two reasons. First, we fight for the workers and they appreciate it. Second, we believe in organization. We have arms and legs in Shell and Stanvac, subdivided into groups of twenty or thirty. Each group is led by a chairman, elected by the members. The chairman represents his group in all dealings with the company. At least once a month, sometimes twice, it is his duty to meet the company's manager and make some demand for the workers. Whether it is for better overalls, or a cleaner toilet, or anything else he can think of, he must show the workers that Perbum is always on the job.

"Every week the group has an evening meeting. It discusses current problems and receives instructions from above. It doesn't waste time with the Koran. It sticks to reality. First, grievances. Second, methods of overcoming the company's unwillingness to meet our demands. Third, the whole situation of labor in Indonesia."

Simandjuntak went on to describe that situation. "As the nation's economy goes down, so do the living standards of the worker. Why is our economy so bad? Because it is practically all in the hands of Dutch, American and British imperialists. The imperialists try to cover this up. For instance, they set up NION, nominally a mixed Shell-Indonesian company. But actually, the oil is controlled by Shell. We want to stop this. We want an Indonesian on NION's Board of Directors. We want nationalization of all oil that has been developed since Independence. We want to control production and distribution ourselves. In that way, we will no longer be at Shell's and Stanvac's mercy."

"Look, Simandjuntak," the labor official interrupted, "you know very well there is nothing unmerciful about Stanvac and Shell."

"I know," said Simandjuntak, "that Stanvac and Shell are draining our land each year of twelve million tons of precious oil. They extract from us an annual profit of over six billion rupiahs. Our workers may not understand the meaning of such big numbers. But they understand this—that the standard of living about which America boasts is high precisely because ours is low. Each time your propagandists flaunt your cars, telephones and beauty parlors, you remind us that we are footing the bill. When all the farmers and workers of Indonesia know the truth, such abuses will be ended. They are learning the truth too. If you doubt me, come to one of our meetings."

I promised Simandjuntak that I would. After he left, I asked the labor official the relative strength of the unions. "Five per cent of the workers," he said, "belong to the Islamic Union, seventy per cent belong to Perbum."

✿   ✿   ✿

Banners across the road and posters on the walls announced the Communist Party rally. Buses had picked up workers and village people and had deposited them by the hundreds at the football field where the meeting was held. A platform, guarded by smartly groomed members of the All-Indonesian Veterans' Association, stood in midfield. Speakers looked out benevolently upon the gathering. All wore the black velvet caps of loyal Indonesians, except one whose white hat and beard proclaimed a holy man. A band played the national anthem. Solemnly, speakers and audience sang the moving words.

The hadji then raised his hands to heaven and begged Allah's blessing on all who loved their native land, who struggled against outsiders' interference, and who worked for the freedom and prosperity of the people. All good Moslems and Communists, he proclaimed, wanted the same thing, peace.

Another speaker took the microphone.

"You have just heard a respected hadji pray to God. Do you believe your own eyes and ears, or do you believe the agents of imperialism who tell you communism is against God? Whoever truly understands the words of the Prophet knows that Islam and communism are one. That Mohammed's love of the common people, the workers and the farmers, is the love of the Communist too. That the Prophet's struggle against wealth and exploitation is the struggle of our party."

The speaker pointed to the flag. "Is this the flag of a foreign power—or of Indonesia? 'Indonesia Raja' our national anthem—or do we sing the hymn of a foreign land? Who upholds the noble principles of the Pantjasila more faithfully than we Communists? How can anyone truthfully say we serve a foreign power? Communism was born in Indonesia's *rukun desas*. Communism's creed is expressed in its slogan, *Gotong rojong*—let us do it together! Communism in Indonesia is *Indonesian* com-

191

munism. Unlike capitalism and imperialism, it is a means of serving *our* nation, *our* people!"

The next speaker was Simandjuntak.

"Our philosophy," he said, "springs directly from the history of our land. We were a colony of a Western country for many centuries. The *belandas* were rich. Our own standard of living was low. We had no social security. Our labor was the cheapest in the world. Yet our country was one of the richest. I myself have seen the world. I have been to the Soviet Union. Our country is as rich as Russia. We have climate, minerals, food, everything to make us rich. Yet the Soviet people are better off than we.

"In Russia, the outstanding thing is good human relationships. A man can talk freely there. The government encourages criticism of everything. When I visited the oil regions, I heard workers freely criticize the quality of their tools and boots. Can they do more than criticize—can they strike? Certainly the Communist worker and peasant can strike. But does it make sense for someone to strike against himself? Why should an engineer go on strike, or try to damage his own engine or railroad? Strikes are for capitalist and colonial countries.

"I saw no beggars or prostitutes in Russia. As for the oil workers, let me say this. If the lowest-paid worker in Russia gets an index of one tenth of one, the director of the whole refinery gets five or six. In Indonesia, if the lowest one gets one tenth of one, the director gets one hundred thirty.

"Capitalist countries have noble constitutions and fine-sounding laws. But there is no connection between law and reality. In Russia, law and reality are identical. A draft of each new law is discussed by the people. After it is passed, it represents their own desires, and they obey it.

"Can a true democracy be governed by only one party?

America has two parties, in Indonesia we have thirty. Does that mean that we are more democratic than America? The number of parties in a country is no index of its democracy. One good party, if it stands for the people, is enough.

"America claims it is a democracy. It boasts of its free enterprise. What is free enterprise but the right of one man to overpower another? Its free-enterprise system, applied to the world, makes it the greatest imperialist of modern times. Free enterprise enables America to come here and drain our land each year of twelve million tons of precious oil. It enables foreign companies to take from us an annual profit of six billion, six hundred million rupiahs! Seventy per cent of our country is still owned by outsiders—Dutch, American, British imperialists. They own our rubber, our tin, our oil, our tea, our harbors and estates. We want to drive them out and to own and share our country's wealth ourselves.

"How? Our method is to organize the people. One, labor must be organized. It must be a pushing power. Two, farmers must be organized. Three, add labor and farmers together, and the sum is a powerful push. Also, intellectuals, youth, women, religion, national enterprise must be organized. *Organization is basic to success!*"

A last speaker drove home the rally's crucial point:

"Did you shed your blood for *merdeka*—independence? Yes! Did you win political independence? Yes! But are you yourself better off? Are all men equal? Are the poor as good as the rich? The answer is no! *Merdeka* has been sold out to America and the imperialist powers! *Merdeka, independence, is not enough!*

"What every patriotic Indonesian wants is *bebas*—the *personal* independence on which freedom depends. For the country to be free, each one of us must be free. Not only politically free, but personally free. That is the goal of the Communist

193

Party. To rid the country of imperialism. To end corruption. To seize power for the people. To win the revolution. To bring to each and every loyal Indonesian the one absolute essential of prosperity and peace—*bebas!*"

As the meeting broke up, a group of workers surrounded me, each drowning out the others' words, so that I could not understand them. One finally quelled the others. "What do you think, *belanda?*" he demanded. "If you were an Indonesian, would you too not join our ranks?" The others waited for my answer.

I shook my head. "I too have been to the Soviet Union. I do not think communism would suit a people like your own, who believe in God, to whom the ownership of an *ubin* of land is so dear, and to whom the family is so precious. I do not think people who lived so long under the strict rule of the Dutch and the Japanese would like to live under another dictatorship. People who believe devoutly in a world of the spirit and to whom Arjuna and Kresno mean so much would not enjoy living in a completely materialistic society. If these are the values your people most prize, you would be wrong to give them up for Communist promises. Communism would be no better for the Indonesian people than for the Russians or Chinese, who are slaves, not masters, of the totalitarian Communist state."

"You mean America's system would be better?"

"No," I said. "I mean the evolution of Indonesia's own system, under Allah and the Pantjasila."

SEVENTEEN

In the Heart of America

W E LEFT SOLO one morning at dawn. Despite the hour, Samiek came to say goodbye with all four of his wives, each lovelier than the other, a multitude of children, and a brother-in-law who drove a bus for a Chinese syndicate. It was he, we learned at the last moment, who comprised Samiek's secret underground, carrying messages to and from far-flung kampongs. Bambang, for the first and only time, dropped his bluff professional manner and wept as we shook hands. I gave my watch to Seneng's father. It was all he would accept for the endless hours he had given Jill. Djogo and Rahaju were also among the many dear, loyal friends who came from great distances to press Jill and Arthur to their breasts, and gifts into our hands. Rahaju whispered to Eadie that she was pregnant. Djogo confided that he had broken with his Communist neighbor for seeking to make political capital of Djogo's personal misfortunes. "I am a simple man," he said, "but I am not blind to his tricks."

Sindo was disconsolate, but he managed to put America's problem in Asia in perfect perspective. "Such good people," he said to Samiek. "What a pity they are *belandas!*" Naioka gave Eadie an embrocation of *tjraken* to guard against miscarriage,

195

and to me she presented a *sate dukun,* the hottest of goat-meat barbecues. Only one friend was missing. As we drove past the prison, we bade Atmo a silent farewell.

We came home to our New Hampshire hills. Neighbors dropped in to tell us what had happened in our absence. The village had built a new school. "Paying for it with our own taxes," said the Selectman. "Built it with our own hands. It's *our* school, to run the way we want."

Eleven children were found to be undernourished. "The problem," said the Women's Club president, "wasn't feeding them. Goodness knows there's food aplenty. But once they knew it was charity, they wouldn't touch it. So the club set out hot lunches for *all* the children. That way everyone eats the same and feels the same. I always say you've got to pay as much account to folks' pride as to their stomachs."

Money for the hot-lunch program had been raised at the annual Summer Fair. "We took in almost five hundred dollars," said the minister's wife. "But we gave good value for what we got. It made us mighty proud to see the summer people snap up our homemade pies and hooked rugs. As long as folks give as good as they get, they can look each other in the eye."

Ralph Sawyer, the handyman, admitted the summer people's money helped the village. All the same, he didn't like them. "Too pushy," he complained. "Always in a hurry. Always tellin' me what to do an' how to do it. Ofttimes when they called, I'd say I couldn't come. Goin' fishin', I'd say, an' hang up. Rather starve than let 'em think they own me!"

Then they asked about our trip. What kind of folks were the Asians? What was wrong out there? Why was Indonesia in such hot water? Why weren't we making better headway? What did the Commies have that we didn't? Wasn't there some big,

196

bold, new idea that could turn the tide in Asia? How could we *win?*

We hesitated to generalize about all of Asia on the basis of our Indonesian experience. Nor did we want to confuse matters by going into the complexities of Indonesian politics, dissidence, civil war and worse. But in certain respects, we felt, what we had learned in Indonesia corresponded to what we knew of other Asian countries and cultures. We tried to answer our neighbors' questions fully and frankly.

We said the Indonesians we'd met were a lot like them, our New Hampshire neighbors. Just as proud, as self-respecting, as chary about charity. Simple on the surface. Shrewd underneath, with a political sense honed sharp as any Yankee's on the rock of experience. Easygoing, but cool toward strangers with big pocketbooks and pushy ways. Eager to get along and live better, but cautious about change. Dead set against being told by outsiders what to think and do. Little farmers and businessmen, mostly, and private enterprisers, like ourselves—folks who liked to match wits in a deal as equals. But joiners too, in all kinds of business, civic and social organizations like our Grange, Rotary and Masons. By and large, a good people, family-loving and God-fearing. Anxious to work out their own solutions to their own problems. Determined to run their own country in their own way. Hopeful for peace and prosperity. Unwilling to buy these at the price of freedom. But, like ourselves, mortal men, sometimes gullible and taken in by clever talk and handsome promises.

We said that, from what we'd seen in Indonesia, not everything America was doing in Asia was wrong. America's policy seemed consistent with the same common-sense principle that led the Women's Club to feed our hungry children. It conformed to our belief in the right of peoples to rule themselves.

197

It was rooted in solid self-interest. Basically, it aimed at lifting living standards, strengthening and stabilizing free and orderly government, making people less vulnerable to communism, keeping Asia's doors open for trade and travel, the free exchange of ideas and goods.

We were lucky, moreover, in the kind of Americans working for us in Asia. The Embassy set, the USIS and ICA technicians, the missionaries, the foundation people, the businessmen we'd met in Indonesia were a hard-working, dedicated group, making heavy personal sacrifices in home life and health to convince Asians of our peaceful character and constructive intent. And not without success.

America was still widely admired and respected. Hundreds of Indonesians we'd known cherished one dream—to visit America. Even criticism of America didn't altogether mean Asia disliked or distrusted us. People didn't talk that way unless they thought it was safe. Deep down, we guessed, most Asians realize they have less to fear from America than from Russia and Red China.

Above all, honest realism underscored the fact that with the best will in the world, America couldn't save Asia, Indonesia or any other country. Only the people of that region, in the long run, could save themselves. Whatever happened in a country like Indonesia, for instance, was largely beyond the reach of American policy and action.

America, moreover, had an uphill row to hoe in Asia. Asians had bitter memories of white, Western rule. This rule was identified with mercantilism, an early form of capitalism conspicuous in the East. Some of Asia's fear, suspicion and even hatred was bound to rub off on us. America, too, was a self-tagged member of something called "the West." We had economic, military and cultural ties with European countries associated, in

Asian minds, with past humiliation. We must expect every friendly act toward the Netherlands, for instance, to arouse Indonesian ire. At the moment, foreign policy acceptable to both Asia and Europe simply wasn't in the cards. Nor could America, even if it tried, hide its imperfections. When these touched on race, as in Little Rock, they touched Asia to the quick.

Colonialism, color, old-fashioned, predatory capitalism, identification with a "Western Bloc" in a struggle hopelessly misnamed "East versus West" were made-to-order issues for the Kremlin. And communism was not without clever, vindictive, mistaken or unmoral disciples hidden among Asia's masses, who used them to our disadvantage.

Why weren't we making better headway in Asia? Mainly, we thought, because America had been led astray by a series of dubious assumptions. To name a few:

1) Asians are illiterate—therefore ignorant, backward and poor. (The Indonesians we'd met counted themselves knowledgeable, advanced in many respects, and rich. Rich in culture. Rich in spirituality. Rich in human experience. Rich in many ways they deemed more important than money.)

2) Asians covet the material wealth of the West and want to emulate Western dynamism. (Most of the Indonesians we'd known didn't want cars or atomic energy so much as a better buffalo or bicycle. They didn't envy Western dynamism. What they wanted might be called "Eastern dynamism," the development and improvement of their own cherished institutions and familiar techniques, rather than replacement of those institutions and techniques by Western substitutes.)

3) Western science is superior to Asia's. (For all their need of Western medicine, Indonesians valued their own concept of science, embracing God, man, the supernatural as well as the

199

rational, as more inclusive and advanced than purely physical science. Few attitudes, indeed, irritated Indonesians more than any assumption of Western superiority.)

4) Asians leaned on Western philosophies of government, either Jeffersonianism, or Marxism, or Fabianism. (While it was true, unfortunately, that Marxism and communism had insinuated themselves into Asian nationalism and had many Asian adherents, Asians, in the main, wanted to evolve their own philosophies. In instruments like their Pantjasila, for example, Indonesians found a philosophy broader, more humanistic, more advanced and satisfying than "tired" Western expressions of government. They sought as much respect for their political beliefs as we do for ours.)

5) The world seeks leadership. It is America's destiny, at this moment in history, to provide it. (To people so recently released from white, Western leadership, any such assumption was intolerable. Asians wanted co-operation, partnership, a sharing of responsibility with others, on a basis of utter equality. If leadership were to come from any outside source, they preferred the United Nations to any single foreign power.)

6) Because a program is good in motive, and productive of material result, Asians will so accept it. (Asians, with different values than ours, judged ideas, motives and results by their own standards. They were conditioned to expect in even the most benign action by white Westerners a benefit to white Westerners. Only programs with built-in answers, expressed in Asian terms and values, could correct this distortion. Only great good judgment could prevent any benefit not immediately available to all Asians from arousing envy, resentment and unrest among those to whom, even temporarily, the benefit was denied.)

7) Our official information services were set up to create Asian understanding of America; it was their job to do so;

200

Asia's hostility toward us proved the ineptness of our official efforts. (Actually, Asians to whom such services as our libraries and cultural-exchange facilities were available profited in better appreciation of America, although not always overtly. Few, however, were reached by our official services. Most judged America on the evidence presented in our commercially distributed films, news services and publications.)

8) A final dubious assumption was that dollars can modernize Asia, hold communism at bay, and make Asia safe for our kind of democracy. (Dollars are important. But in Indonesia we learned that unless dollars were wisely managed, they often wound up in the pockets of the most predatory members of the community. By worsening inflation and widening inequality, dollars sometimes invited the very evils they were intended to allay. Nothing could be more mistaken than to think psychological or political results could be achieved by purely material means. Unless America understood—and helped develop—Asia's *human* potential as well as its agricultural and industrial potential, all our wealth and technical know-how, poured heedlessly into Asia, might ultimately wind up in Communist hands.)

Each of these assumptions was packed with psychological dynamite. Every word or action resting on them was explosive. America, indeed, was often rocked by such explosions. Some of them, as in China, were so large and loud they still echoed in our ears. More often, they were so small, so silent, they damaged only the heart or spirit of the Asian affected.

What of some big, bold, new idea that could turn the tide in Asia? We told our neighbors we hadn't been able to think of any. All we could think of were little ideas like those our neighbors had been telling us about our New England village: Its pride in building its own school, unbeholden, to run as it

201

wanted. Its consideration for the self-respect of its smallest child. The determination of its poorest citizens not to be "owned" by others. Its ability to satisfy village needs by satisfying the wants of the summer people. The common sense that underlay its decisions and dealings one with another.

America's strength flowed from these little things. Awareness of the importance of people. Knowledge of how human beings feel, think, act. Skill in building pride and preserving self-respect. Ability in fusing purposes and actions into common enterprises for the common good. Tact, grace, consideration in intercourse among its many different races, creeds and colors. We were far from perfect in these matters. But, basically, it was to these qualities that our society constantly aspired.

The strength of America's economy was drawn from the same sources. American industry recognized the consumer's importance as paramount. It carefully studied his needs, tastes, taboos. It lavished infinite care on their satisfaction. It synthesized consumer self-interest with its own. It showed endless concern for a peculiarly American science called "public relations." It rarely spent a dollar without anticipating some specific, constructive result. These same principles were reflected in management's relations with labor.

Somehow, these, the commonplace qualities of our society and the essence of our power, spiritual and material, deserted us in our dealings with Asians.

These, America's commonplace qualities, were needed to win the struggle for the peace, justice, prosperity and freedom America wanted for itself and for others.

The President of the United States had clearly defined the nature of that struggle.

"The great struggle of our times," said Dwight Eisenhower, "is one of the spirit. It is a struggle for the hearts and souls of men—not merely for property or even merely for power. It is a contest for the beliefs, the convictions, the very innermost soul of the human being."

Such a struggle could not be won by the United States Government. It could not be won by feats of arms, nor by billions of dollars. It could be won only by Americans acting toward others with the same common sense that marked their dealings among themselves. It could not be won by "bold diplomacy." It could be won only by showing toward others precisely the same consideration and respect for human pride and dignity we demanded for ourselves. It could not be won by propaganda. It could be won only by human understanding *at the rice roots.*

Americans did not tactlessly and persistently refer to any segment of our own society as backward, illiterate, diseased, ignorant, poverty-stricken and undeveloped. Our method was to exalt, rather than to diminish people's self-respect and pride, while correcting the faults that afflicted them. Why, then, should we behave so differently toward Asians?

Americans preferred honest deals and fair exchanges to the inferior status implicit in "aid." Our federal and state grants were usually matched, in whole or part, by the segment of our society favored. Our philanthropy took care lest, in succoring human need, it debased human dignity. Why, then, a "something for nothing" approach to Asians? Why, in technical programs abroad, such sole reliance on scientific criteria as opposed to human criteria? In terms of Indonesia's crisis, why greater concern for the physical properties of Sumatra's *land* than for the political and economic pressures on Indonesia's *people?*

Americans moved gradually toward betterment in our own society. Though we worked toward the development of atomic power, we pitched our daily lives to our existing environment, contenting ourselves with little improvements we felt we could afford. We preferred moderation and persuasion to abrupt transition. Why, then, conjure before Asians scientific dreams we have not yet realized ourselves?

Americans didn't trample on each other's beliefs. We were careful how we sought to influence each other. We knew the folly of assuming superior airs and preaching sermons. We appealed to people in terms of their own self-interest. Why not similar understanding, consideration and respect for Asian beliefs and feelings?

Americans didn't elect anyone to captain a team because he assumed his right to leadership. Leadership was a quality we sensed in others, usually in terms of some benefit to the led. Leadership was an honor we conferred, as a reward for skills we ourselves acknowledged and appreciated. America prized sovereignty and independence. Americans wanted neither to follow foreign leaders nor to lead foreign serfs. Why then, to Asians, so much talk of American leadership?

America's politicians strove mightily to plumb the mood of their humblest constituents. American business went to incredible lengths in searching out the customers' tastes. America's avant-garde in technology, education, the arts took care not to lose contact with the people. No one knew better than Americans that before an idea could capture the hearts and souls of men, or a product could capture their purses, it must first become identified with the masses. It was not in America's character to be indifferent to the multitudes, nor to lose contact with them, nor to underestimate their intelligence, ability and common sense. Why, then, the gulf between Americans and Asia's masses? Why an approach solely toward Asia's elite? Why the constant need to conduct our Asian affairs over the Asian people's heads?

Americans believed in voluntary co-operation among people

204

or agencies pursuing common goals. They believed in singling out fields where action was logical and proper, and focusing their efforts on these. They judged success not alone in material terms, but in abstractions like good will. Why, then, competition among American agencies, private and public, to solve Asia's problems? Why the scattering of our efforts, the lack of concentration in legitimate, natural, important fields like English-language teaching? Why such stress on material means, such neglect of social, psychological and political ends?

Americans loved movies as distraction, entertainment and escape. They were troubled, too, by the impact of certain pictures on audiences unable to evaluate them correctly. Americans took regulatory action when comic books and other less admirable aspects of our literary output offended good taste. Americans generally expected the agencies responsible to correct their abuses of our traditional freedoms, especially when such abuses were against the public good. Why, then, such blithe disregard of the power, responsibility and opportunity of our commercial news and entertainment channels in Asia?

Americans knew that dollars hadn't built America. What built America was the imagination, will power, sacrifice and sweat of its people. Dollars hadn't bought our freedom. America's freedom grew out of great ideas. Dollars did not protect our freedom. America's freedom had been defended with the blood of men to whom freedom was more precious than life. Why, then, the eternal argument over how many billions for foreign aid—and the eternal silence on the *human* factors that, far more than money, will decide Asia's destiny?

Americans, admittedly a pretty rudely vital people, believed in doing to others what they would have others do to them. To win the struggle for the hearts and minds of men, America might best begin by applying that code to Asians.

205

Once we did, many things might happen.

We'd take as much as we gave. Not alone rubber, tin and oil, but the products of Asia's craftsmen and cottage workers.

Our schools and universities would broaden their Asian courses. Libraries and stores would widen their range of Asian books. Statesmen and others who speak for America would broaden their vision of Asia and, without minimizing its problems, pay tribute to its greatness and heed to its pride. Our educators, librarians and publishers would know that Asians are starving—starving for books, for knowledge, for self-respect and the respect of others that education commands. Americans would recognize this hunger—the forgotten hunger of a Lincoln for a printed page—and act to satisfy it. America would act with awareness that man does not live by bread alone.

Our economists would act to strengthen Asia's indigenous economic institutions, bolstering village collectives, co-operatives and banks, and broadening rural credit. They would encourage Asia's small private entrepreneurs. They would appreciate the efforts of Asia's little people to build their own growth economy and generate their own capital. They would show no hostility toward socialism, collectivism, welfarism. They would stress, instead, the popular nature of modern capitalism, tailoring it not alone to giant dams, atomic reactors, the exigencies of international trade, but to the stature of Asia's village economy. That America itself has a highly collectivized welfare economy would not be hidden.

Our official and private agencies would determine the few, specific fields in which America can act logically and legitimately in Asia. When, as in Indonesia, the English language has been chosen as the nation's first foreign language, we would co-ordinate and concentrate our funds and skills to meet the opportunity and challenge. We would apply our merchandising

talents to textbooks, reference books, worth-while fiction, training aids and teaching devices. We would make our language
useful in solving Asia's problems, rather than in corrupting its
youth or defaming America.

Our private and federal agencies, while expanding the benefits of Western medicine to the fullest, would also help improve
Asia's existing indigenous medical base, however strange it
seems. They would work beside Asia's midwives, nurses, witch
doctors, *sages-femmes* and *dukuns,* broadening their usefulness
throughout the decades it will take to train doctors and to build
clinics adequate to Asia's needs. They would appreciate, and
learn from, Asia's metaphysicians.

American corporations in Asia, especially those engaged in
extractive activities, would offer laboratories, equipment and
scientific training to Asia's schools in exchange for the services
of their graduates. They would set their records straight with
their workers, in language their employees understood. They
would send no American abroad without thorough instruction
in Asian culture and character. With skill born of sensitivity,
they would expunge the fantastic falsehoods of Communist
dupes. They would pay heed to the power of organization applied, not simply to science and technology, but to human impulses and social forces.

American agencies and corporations in Asia would lean heavily on our anthropologists and social scientists for guidance.
They would work with the grain of Asian culture, rather than
cut across it. They would act with awareness that every action
undermining, replacing or reforming Asia's culture invites resentment and creates the very rootlessness, restlessness, discon-
tent and insecurity we seek to prevent. They would not wait for
unrest and civil war, as in Indonesia, to signal social ills.
Plumbing the deeper currents at the rice roots, sensing the ten-

sions slowly but surely building up, they would apply what influence they had to preventive action.

We would know that America's dynamic culture, exported, ceases to be strictly business, or simply art, or merely entertainment, but the most important single factor in winning or losing Asia's confidence, respect and friendship.

America would know that its reputation is made largely by its movies. Hollywood would not interpret this as insult or attack, but as acknowledgement of its success, its power, its responsibility. It would insist on *objective* studies of its impact on Asians, especially those with no criteria by which to judge America other than Hollywood's vivid image. Hollywood would be responsive to the facts. Not by censorship, but by consciously aiming to produce one picture in ten, perhaps, truly reflective of the real America.

America would vastly expand its information *services* to Asia, emphasis being on service, not propaganda. Nor would America's commercial news services and publishers remain unmoved by the responsibility presented by our predicament in Asia. America's writers and artists, too, would awaken to the drama implicit in so vital a theme. Books, plays, short stories, perhaps, would cast the light of creative insight on as crucial a problem as has challenged the talent of man.

The list of what America's housewives, merchants, tourists, teachers, doctors, clergymen, impresarios, authors, engineers, and other private citizens would do was as long as America's vision and as infinite as its genius. Unions, women's clubs, pen pals, professional groups would lay two-way lines to their opposite numbers in Asia. Statesmen would speak less of leadership than of willingness to work side by side with others to achieve legitimate aims. Citizens without their own direct channels of action would seek out and support our private agencies

208

operating in Asia. Americans, all, would gladly grant the one thing Asians want more than machinery, money, know-how, progress, prosperity and peace itself—*equality*.

The American people would realize that times change and so do administrations. That situations vary, and so do solutions. That programs, policies, plans and panaceas shift with each new wind that blows from Asia, and none endures. That all that endures is the character of a people.

America was searching for the way to win the struggle for the hearts and souls of men.

Down deep at its own grass roots was where America would find it.

In its President's words: "Whatever America hopes to bring to pass in the world must first come to pass in the heart of America."

ABOUT THE AUTHOR

Shortly after completing this book, ARTHUR GOODFRIEND *accepted an appointment as Public Affairs Officer for the United States Information Agency in New Delhi, India. This was his sixth trip to Asia. Previously he had lived in other parts of that vast continent as a businessman, as a government official, and as a plain American trying to understand people at the "rice roots." Between Asian visits he makes his home in New Hampshire.*